SHORT WAL
MADE EASY

COTSWOLDS

Ordnance Survey

Contents

Getting outside in the Cotswolds		6
We smile more when we're outside		8
Respecting the countryside		10
Using this guide		11
Walk 1	Hidcote	**14**
Walk 2	Off Broadway	**20**
Photos	Scenes from the walks	26
Walk 3	Sudeley Castle	**28**
Walk 4	Bourton-on-the-Water	**34**
Photos	Wildlife interest	40
Walk 5	Cornbury Park	**42**
Walk 6	Blenheim Park	**48**
Walk 7	Bibury	**54**
Photos	Cafés and pubs	60
Walk 8	Cirencester Park	**62**
Walk 9	Chalford	**68**
Walk 10	Woodchester Park	**74**
Credits		80

Map symbols	Front cover flap
Accessibility and what to take	Back cover flap
Walk locations	Inside front cover
Your next adventure?	Inside back cover

2 Short Walks Made Easy

Walk 1
HIDCOTE

Distance
3 miles / 4.9km

Time
1½ hours

Start/Finish
Hidcote

Parking GL55 6LR
Hidcote car park (NT)

Cafés/pubs
Winthrop's Café (NT)

World-class gardens inspired by Arts and Crafts movement

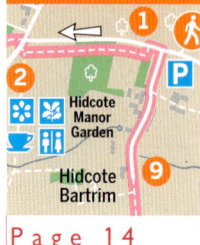

Page 14

Walk 2
OFF BROADWAY

Distance
4.1 miles/6.6km
Time
2 hours *CATCH A BUS*
Start/Finish
Broadway

Parking WR12 7AH
Church Close car park

Cafés/pubs
Broadway

Sumptuous Cotswolds views, a sleepy hamlet and tempting tearooms

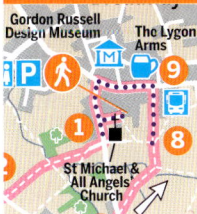

Page 20

Walk 3
SUDELEY CASTLE

Distance
1.6 miles/2.6km
Time
1¼ hours *CATCH A BUS*
Start/Finish
Winchcombe

Parking GL54 5HX
Bull Lane car park

Cafés/pubs
The Pavilion, Sudeley Castle; Winchcombe

Historic stately home, fine gardens and picnic site; meteorite debris

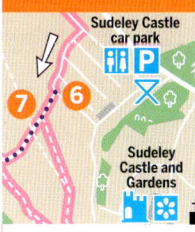

Page 28

Walk 4
BOURTON-ON-THE-WATER

Distance
4.1 miles/6.6km
Time
2 hours *CATCH A BUS*
Start/Finish
Bourton-on-the-Water

Parking GL54 2LU
Bourton Vale car park

Cafés/pubs
Bourton-on-the-Water

Charming and popular millstream village; glorious meadows

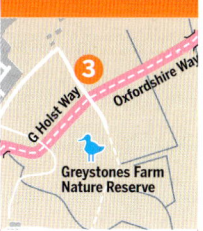

Page 34

Contents 3

Walk 5

CORNBURY PARK

Distance
2.1 miles/3.3km

Time
1 hour

Start Finstock
Finish Charlbury

Parking OX7 3PQ
Spendlove Centre car park, Charlbury

Cafés/pubs
Café and pubs in Charlbury; pub in Finstock

Beautiful deer parkland, sycamore avenues and Charlbury glove-making

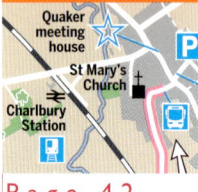

Page 42

Walk 6

BLENHEIM PARK

Distance
4.1 miles/6.6km

Time
2 hours

Start/Finish
Woodstock

Parking OX20 1JF
Union Street car park, Hensington Road

Cafés/pubs
Blenheim Palace; Woodstock

A grand house, gardens and maze at a UNESCO World Heritage Site

Page 48

Walk 7

BIBURY

Distance
1.8 miles/2.9km

Time
1 hour

Start/Finish
Bibury

Parking GL7 5NL
Village lay-by, opposite Bibury Trout Farm

Cafés/pubs
The Swan Hotel; The Catherine Wheel pub

Charming village walk, passing England's most photographed cottages

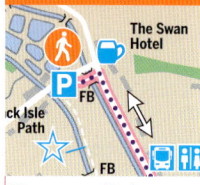

Page 54

Walk 8

CIRENCESTER PARK

Distance
3 miles/4.8km

Time
1½ hours

Start/Finish
Cirencester

Parking GL7 1HN
Sheep Street car park

Cafés/pubs
Kiosk in Cirencester Park; Cirencester

Expansive park views; Roman town; world's tallest yew hedge

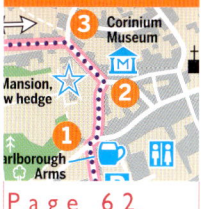

Page 62

Walk 9

CHALFORD

Distance
2.8 miles/4.6km

Time
1½ hours

Start/Finish
Chalford

Parking GL6 8PP
A419, London Road, long lay-by

Cafés/pubs
Lavender Bakehouse and Coffee Shop

Lush flora and fauna, canal heritage; coffee shop and pub en route

Page 68

Walk 10

WOODCHESTER PARK

Distance
3.5 miles/5.6km

Time
1¾ hours

Start/Finish
Woodchester Park

Parking GL10 3TS
Woodchester Park car park (NT)

Cafés/pubs
Woodchester Mansion café (when house is open)

Away-from-it-all wooded valley and lakes; Gothic mansion

Page 74

Contents 5

GETTING OUTSIDE IN THE COTSWOLDS

" "

I hope you enjoy using this series of short walks exploring this chocolate-box-pretty region of Great Britain

OS Champion
Zoe Homes

Broadway Tower

A very warm welcome to the new Short Walks Made Easy guide to the Cotswolds — what a fantastic selection of leisurely walks we have for you here!

The Cotswolds conjure up images of honey-coloured stone cottages, lush rolling hills, and deeply cut wooded valleys. The name is apt, originating from a Saxon term meaning 'wooded hollows amid gentle hills'. The Cotswolds Area of Outstanding Natural Beauty was designated back in 1966 and is the largest AONB in the country, covering over 780 square miles between Stratford-upon-Avon and Bath, and straddling six counties: predominantly Gloucestershire and Oxfordshire, but also Warwickshire, Wiltshire, Worcestershire and Somerset.

Quieter corners are explored alongside some of the region's popular highlights. For quintessential Cotswold views, follow the trail from Broadway or stroll down Broad Ride in Cirencester Park. At the charming old millstream village of Bourton-on-the-Water you can enjoy a post-walk ice cream, while on the outing from Bibury, have your camera ready to snap the country's most-photographed cottages at Arlington Row.

In addition to admiring formal gardens at the stately homes of Sudeley Castle and Blenheim Palace, you can relax in the Arts and Crafts-inspired planting at Hidcote. The beautifully wooded valley of Woodchester Park and the ancient deer parkland at Cornbury offer away-from-it-all rambles, and don't miss the waterside wildlife-spotting opportunities along the Thames and Severn Canal from Chalford.

I hope you enjoy using this series of short walks exploring this chocolate-box-pretty region of Great Britain.

Zoe Homes, OS Champion

WE SMILE MORE WHEN WE'RE OUTSIDE

Bourton-on-the-Water

Whether it's a short walk during our lunch break or a full day's outdoor adventure, we know that a good dose of fresh air is just the tonic we all need.

At Ordnance Survey (OS), we're passionate about helping more people to get outside more often. It sits at the heart of everything we do, and through our products and services, we aim to help you lead an active outdoor lifestyle, so that you can live longer, stay younger and enjoy life more.

We firmly believe the outdoors is for everyone, and we want to help you find the very best Great Britain has to offer. We are blessed with an island that is beautiful and unique, with a rich and varied landscape. There are coastal paths to meander along, woodlands to explore, countryside to roam, and cities to uncover. Our trusted source of inspirational content is bursting with ideas for places to go, things to do and easy beginner's guides on how to get started.

It can be daunting when you're new to something, so we want to bring you the know-how from the people who live and breathe the outdoors. To help guide us, our team of awe-inspiring OS Champions share their favourite places to visit, hints and tips for outdoor adventures, as well as tried and tested accessible, family- and wheelchair-friendly routes. We hope that you will feel inspired to spend more time outside and reap the physical and mental health benefits that the outdoors has to offer. With our handy guides, paper and digital mapping, and exciting new apps, we can be with you every step of the way.

To find out more visit os.uk/getoutside

RESPECTING
THE COUNTRYSIDE

You can't beat getting outside in the British countryside, but it's vital that we leave no trace when we're enjoying the great outdoors.

Let's make sure that generations to come can enjoy the countryside just as we do.

 Leave no trace

 Keep dogs under control; bin and bag waste

 Do not light fires; only BBQ at official sites

 Leave gates as you find them

 Keep to footpaths and open access land

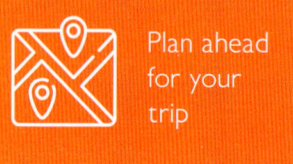 Plan ahead for your trip

For more details please visit
www.gov.uk/countryside-code

USING THIS GUIDE

Easy-to-follow Cotswolds walks for all

Before setting off

Check the walk information panel to plan your outing

- Consider using **Public transport** where flagged. If driving, note the satnav postcode for the car park under **Parking**
- The suggested **Time** is based on a gentle pace
- Note the availability of **Cafés**, tearooms and pubs, and **Toilets**

Terrain and hilliness

- **Terrain** indicates the nature of the route surface
- Any rises and falls are noted under **Hilliness**

Walking with your dog?

- This panel states where **Dogs** must be on a lead and how many stiles there are – in case you need to lift your dog
- Keep dogs on leads where there are livestock and between April and August in forest and on grassland where there are ground-nesting birds

A perfectly pocket-sized walking guide

- Handily sized for ease of use on each walk
- When not being read, it fits nicely into a pocket…
- …so between points, put this book in the pocket of your coat, trousers or day sack and enjoy your stroll in glorious countryside – we've made it pocket-sized for a reason!

Flexibility of route presentation to suit all readers

- **Not comfortable map reading?** Then use the simple-to-follow route profile and accompanying route description and pictures
- **Happy to map read?** New-look walk mapping makes it easier for you to focus on the route and the points of interest along the way
- **Read the insightful Did you know?, Local legend, Stories behind the walk** and **Nature notes** to help you make the most of your day out and to enjoy all that each walk has to offer

Cotswolds 11

OS information about the walk

- Many of the features and symbols shown are taken from Ordnance Survey's celebrated **Explorer** mapping, designed to help people across Great Britain enjoy leisure time spent outside

- National Grid reference for the start point
- Explorer sheet map covering the route

OS information
🚶 SP 177430
Explorer 205

The easy-to-use walk map

- **Large-scale** mapping for ultra-clear route finding

- **Numbered points** at key turns along the route that tie in with the route instructions and respective points marked on the profile

- **Pictorial symbols** for intuitive map reading, see Map Symbols on the front cover flap

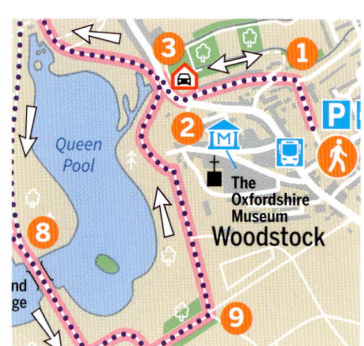

The simple-to-follow walk profile

- Progress easily along the route using the illustrative profile, it has **numbered points** for key turning points and **graduated distance** markers

- Easy-read **route directions** with turn-by-turn detail

- Reassuring **route photographs** for each numbered point

Grand Bridge
(Queen Pool, left;
The Lake, right)
3 miles

7 — **Cross** the bridge and turn **left** in front of the palace gates along a wide tarmac path.

12 Short Walks Made Easy

Using QR codes

- Scan each QR code to see the route in Ordnance Survey's OS Maps App.
NB You may need to download a scanning app if you have an older phone

- OS Maps will open the route automatically if you have it installed. If not, the route will open in the web version of OS Maps

- Please click **Start Route** button to begin navigating or **Download Route** to store the route for offline use

WALK 1

HIDCOTE

It's quite a thing for a small village to possess a fine and internationally renowned garden. But not content with that, just 300 yards up the road, Hidcote Bartrim has the magical Kiftsgate Court (kiftsgate.co.uk) too – a glorious garden created by three generations of women. This walk passes the entrances to both before making a circuit of this bucolic hilltop, passing a moving tribute by a Belgian soldier to his fallen comrade during World War I.

OS information

SP 177430
Explorer 205

Distance
3 miles/4.9km

Time
1½ hours

Start/Finish
Hidcote

Parking GL55 6LR
National Trust
Hidcote car park

Public toilets
Hidcote Manor

Cafés/pubs
Winthrop's Café at Hidcote Manor Garden (NT)

Terrain
Lanes; field, woodland and tarmac paths

Hilliness
One descent to ❸ and short climb beyond

Footwear
Spring/Autumn/Winter 👢
Summer 👞

14 Short Walks Made Easy

Public transport
None

Accessibility
Hidcote Manor Garden is accessible, but the route is not suitable for wheelchairs or pushchairs

Dogs Welcome but keep on leads. Two stiles (one with dog gate; one low stile)

Did you know? Hidcote Manor has a sister garden on the south coast of France. In 1924, Hidcote's creator, Major Lawrence Johnston, bought Serre de la Madone in Menton. He spent his summers at Hidcote and the rest of the year at Menton, where 12 gardeners looked after his exotic plants brought in from the world's subtropical regions. After Johnston's death in 1958 the garden fell into disrepair but has since been restored and opened to the public.

Local legend A mile-long tunnel to the south-west of Hidcote is said to be the site – and indeed the cause – of the very last pitched battle on English soil between two private armies. The opposing sides in July 1851 were several hundred navvies digging the railway tunnel for a contractor, and reportedly up to 3,000 men led by Isambard Kingdom Brunel, who sought to take possession of the tunnel. Numerous injuries were recorded but happily no fatalities.

Walk 1 Hidcote 15

STORIES BEHIND THE WALK

☆ Hidcote Gold

Such is the admiration for Lawrence Johnston and his work that many flowers have been named after Hidcote in his honour. These include roses, lavenders and a dog's tooth violet. One of the roses, called Hidcote Gold, is a shrub that produces long branches covered with brilliant canary-yellow flowers and can bring a joyful taste of Hidcote to humbler gardens.

☆ Arts and Crafts

The Arts and Crafts movement was founded in the 1860s as a reaction to the Industrial Revolution, which had largely replaced decorative objects made by hand with mass-produced artefacts lacking in craftsmanship. The movement's principal driver was William Morris, whose interior decoration business was inspired by the work of craftspeople from the Middle Ages. His compatriots included artist Edward Burne-Jones, architect Augustus Pugin and art critic John Ruskin.

Hidcote car park (NT)

2 Entrance to Kiftsgate Court

½ mile

- Leave the car park by passing the attendant's shelter on your right.
- Walk **ahead** along the lane for 20 yards to a gate and fingerpost on the left.

1
- Use the gate to join the footpath running parallel with the road.
- Continue through a kissing-gate and along the right-hand side of a field until you reach a road.

16 Short Walks Made Easy

☆ **Lawrence Johnston** Born in Paris in 1871 to wealthy American parents, Johnston became a British subject and a soldier, fighting in the Second Boer War. It was in South Africa that he became interested in plants. Moving into his mother's 287-acre Hidcote Manor estate in 1907, he started creating a garden. He travelled widely to find plants for Hidcote and sponsored others to do so too. The result is a captivating array of flora from around the world.

Hidcote Manor Garden

Hidcote became the National Trust's very first garden-only property when it was handed to the charity by Lawrence Johnston in 1948. Perched on a long hilltop, it provides a remarkable insight into the Arts and Crafts movement that inspired it. Although it covers 10.5 acres, much of it is split into numerous intimate 'rooms'. Each one has its own unique character, giving visitors the impression that Hidcote is actually a whole host of gardens in one (hidcote.com).

Lane | Baker's Hill | ☆ Belgian soldier tree | 1½ miles
4 | | |
1 mile | | B a k e r ' s
 | | H i l l
 | | W o o d

3 Footbridge

2 ▸ Turn **right** and almost immediately **left** through a large gate beside the entrance to Kiftsgate Court.
▸ Descend a wide grassy slope between woods on a bridleway, and follow it across successive fields to reach a footbridge to your left.

3 ▸ **Cross** the footbridge and bear **left** to head up through a field.
▸ Ignore two footpaths off to the right, keeping **left** until you come to a lane.

Walk 1 Hidcote 17

NATURE NOTES

Burdock is a robust wayside plant. In summer, its Velcro-like sticky seed heads or burs can attach themselves to clothing and dogs' coats. The flowers are a favourite of painted lady and small tortoiseshell butterflies, while the plant has been mixed with dandelion to produce a delicious drink since medieval days.

Vicia incana, an introduced species, has long strings of purple flowers and is often mistaken for vetch, a fellow legume.

2 miles

Barn

5

6 Lane

4 ▸ **Cross** the lane and head up steps, passing a finely carved bench supported by two bears.
▸ Continue **ahead** through a gate at the top and follow the field-edge path, passing the Belgian soldier tree halfway along, to reach a barn.

5 ▸ Turn **left** in front of the barn onto a crumbling road and then, in a few paces, **right** along a footpath.
▸ Remain on this path for ½ mile to a metal field gate on the edge of Hidcote Boyce.

6 ▸ Go through the gate, **cross** the road and head **up** the lane into the hamlet to a road junction.

18 Short Walks Made Easy

Docks are sturdy plants, with distinctive seed heads, much favoured by house sparrows, and large leaves, which have been used for centuries in herbal remedies, for making dyes and, famously, as an antidote to nettle stings.

Come summer, green alkanet produces brilliant blue flowers. It's a relative of the forget-me-not and was imported from south-western Europe.

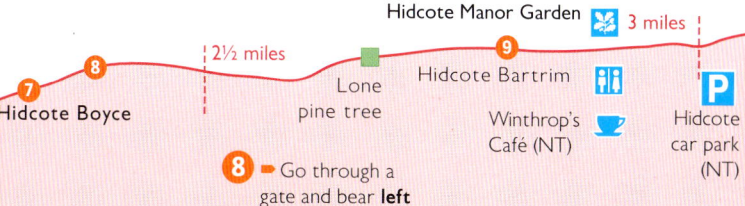

7 Hidcote Boyce — 2½ miles — Lone pine tree — **9** Hidcote Bartrim — Winthrop's Café (NT) — Hidcote Manor Garden — 3 miles — Hidcote car park (NT)

7 ▸ Where the road swings sharp right, continue **ahead** on a narrow lane to its end, passing a spring on your left.

8 ▸ Go through a gate and bear **left** through a field. The path may be faint, so follow the fingerpost direction to a gate which becomes visible in the far hedge.
▸ Continue across another large field, passing a lone pine. Nearing the far side, ignore a path off left and walk to the field corner.

9 ▸ Look for a Monarch's Way waymark in a rose bush to your left.
▸ Step over a low stone stile and keep **forward** along a lane for 400 yards back to the start.

WALK 2

OFF BROADWAY

Broadway is one of the Cotswolds' most visited destinations, made famous by the wide road that runs through it and which lends the large village its name. On this outing you'll be escaping the crowds by heading up a gently sloping hill to the drowsy one-street village of Buckland and its church. From there the walk continues through farmland before taking a path downhill through open fields with sumptuous views of Broadway (with its inviting teashops) on the plain below.

OS information
SP 095373
Explorer OL45

Distance	4.1 miles/6.6km
Time	2 hours
Start/Finish	Broadway
Parking	WR12 7AH Church Close car park
Public toilets	Church Close car park
Cafés/pubs	Broadway
Terrain	Lanes; field, woodland and tarmac paths
Hilliness	One climb, between ③ and ④
Footwear	Spring/Autumn/Winter 🥾 Summer 👟

20 Short Walks Made Easy

Public transport

Bus stops in High St. Bus services 1/1A between Stratford-upon-Avon and Moreton-in-Marsh: stagecoachbus.com; R4 between Evesham and Willersey: nncresswell.co.uk

Accessibility

Around town only; route surfaces not suitable for wheelchairs or pushchairs

Dogs

Welcome, but keep on a lead. Four stiles

Did you know? Broadway is one of Britain's oldest known settlements. Archaeological evidence strongly suggests that there has been human activity here since the Mesolithic era (the middle of the Stone Age), with hunter-gatherers using the location as a base. Much later, the Beaker folk settled the area, followed a couple of millennia later by the Romans. By the time of the Domesday Book – when the village was known as Bradeweia – it was already ancient.

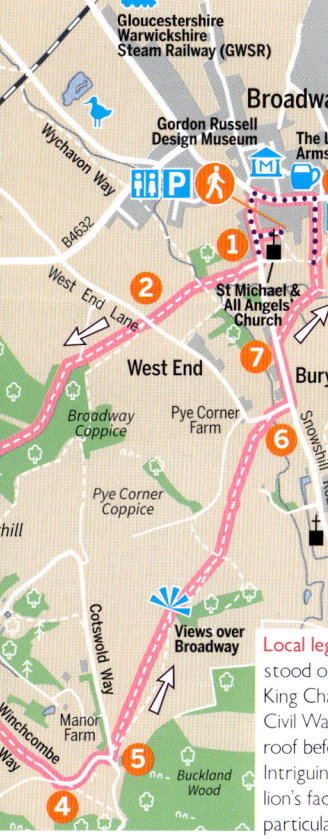

Local legend Evidence suggests that a coaching inn has stood on the site of the Lygon Arms since at least 1377. King Charles I met with his supporters there during the Civil War and Oliver Cromwell spent the night under its roof before meeting success at the Battle of Worcester. Intriguingly, on Charles' coat of arms, still at the hotel, the lion's face has been obliterated. And nobody knows which particular Roundhead did the deed (lygonarmshotel.co.uk).

Walk 2 Off Broadway 21

STORIES BEHIND THE WALK

🏛 Gordon Russell Design Museum
The 12-year-old Gordon Russell moved to Broadway in 1904 when his father bought the Lygon Arms. He soon fell under the spell of the Arts and Crafts movement (see page 16). After winning the Military Cross in World War I, he began producing handcrafted furniture, becoming one of the foremost furniture designers of the 20th century. This fascinating museum tells his story (gordonrusselldesignmuseum.org).

☆ JB Priestley
Famous for its extremely wide High Street, which is also one of the longest in England, Broadway has become a tourist hotspot. However, back in 1933, it somehow failed to impress playwright and author JB Priestley when he visited while researching his hugely successful book, *English Journey*. Of Broadway he wrote, 'The guardian spirits have left this place to its own devices, and those devices are not very pleasing.' It just shows you can't win (over) them all.

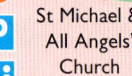
St Michael & All Angels' Church

Church Close car park

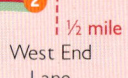
Cotswold Way

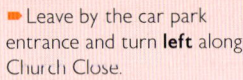
½ mile
West End Lane

1 mile

Broadway Coppice

- Leave by the car park entrance and turn **left** along Church Close.
- At the T-junction turn **left** into Church Street and walk to a Cotswold Way fingerpost 30 yards beyond the church on the right.

① ▶ Go **right** to join the Cotswold Way and follow it, ignoring all side paths, for ⅓ mile to a lane.

22 Short Walks Made Easy

☆ Broadway Tower

At 1,026 feet above sea level, Beacon Hill – on which Broadway Tower stands – is the Cotswolds' second highest peak. In 1588, a fire was lit on the summit to warn of the coming of the Spanish Armada. The tower was conceived by Capability Brown and completed in 1798 to designs by architect James Wyatt. It's a deliberately bizarre concoction of competing castle-like features with sensational views of the Cotswolds countryside from the viewing platform at the top (broadwaytower.co.uk).

🚂 Gloucestershire Warwickshire Steam Railway (GWSR)

Run by volunteers, the GWSR has revived a full 14 miles of the Great Western Railway route from Cheltenham to Birmingham via Stratford-upon-Avon. That line closed in 1976 but a society was immediately formed to preserve the route. By 1984 the first 700 yards of heritage railway was re-opened. Today, it runs from Broadway to Cheltenham Race Course, with four stops in between, crossing the lovely Stanway Viaduct on the way (gwsr.com).

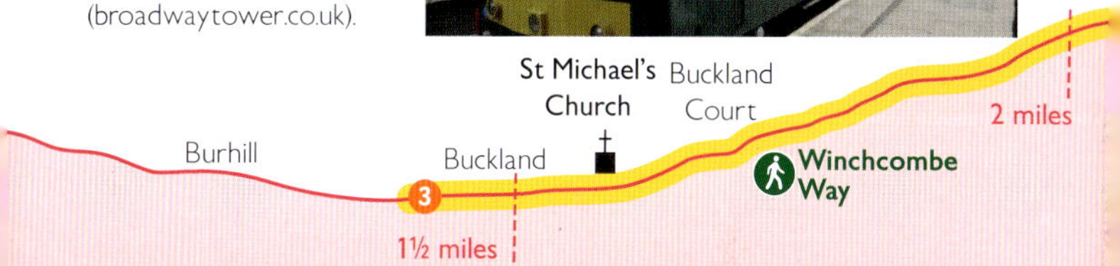

Burhill — Buckland ❸ — St Michael's Church — Buckland Court — 🚶 Winchcombe Way — 2 miles

1½ miles

❷ ▪ **Cross** the road and leave the Cotswold Way, taking a tarmac track to the **right** to head up through Broadway Coppice.
▪ Ignore forks to the left, continuing for almost 1 mile to a row of cottages and then a road.

❸ ▪ Turn **left** to walk through the hamlet of Buckland to a footpath fingerpost on the right, immediately before Buckland Court.
▪ Join the Winchcombe Way, ascending through fields for ½ mile to a main track junction.

Walk 2 Off Broadway

NATURE NOTES

A frequently seen plant of cattle and sheep pasture and the margins of arable fields, common sorrel is recognised by its tall, upright stems and, in May and June, flowers of pink and crimson (see page 40).

The common spotted orchid is one of the more widespread and commonly occurring members of the orchid family. Found on unimproved grassland, its delicate and playful pink hues are always a delight.

Jackdaw

Top: common spotted orchid
Bottom: great horsetail

4 ▶ At a stile with Restricted Byway signs, climb over it then turn **left** (joining the Cotswold Way) and immediately pass through two gates.
▶ Follow this grassy track between fences as it gently descends the hill to a large barn.

5 ▶ Swing **left** at the barn then immediately bear **right** over two stiles, leaving the Cotswold Way.
▶ Continue the descent on a cross-field path, following waymarked posts for ¾ mile over successive fields to reach a kissing-gate and lane.

6 ▶ Pass through the kissing-gate and turn **right** along the lane to a T-junction.
▶ Turn **left**, walking for 300 yards to a stile and fingerpost on the right.

Short Walks Made Easy

In Broadway Coppice, the delicate little herb robert grows alongside the path, in tandem with spectacular clumps of great horsetail.

The jackdaw is the smallest member of the crow family, distinguished by its grey 'bonnet', pale eye and sharp 'jack' call, after which it is named.

In summer, the fields on the way back to Broadway are filled with the pinks and corals of sainfoin, an Asian plant grown for livestock fodder.

Originating in Scotland, the distinctively marked belted Galloway cattle are a hardy breed of livestock, often used for conservation grazing and commercially reared for beef.

West End Lane **6** — Snowshill Road **7** — 3½ miles — **8** — Broadway, High Street **9** — The Lygon Arms — 4 miles — Church Street — Church Close car park

7 ▸ Climb the stile and take the cross-field path and, ignoring side paths and passing a horse jumping arena on your right, reach a waymarked gateway in 400 yards.

8 ▸ Follow the enclosed path before passing between buildings and along a short stretch of road to emerge onto Broadway's High Street.

9 ▸ Head **left** until you reach Church Street.
▸ Turn **left** up it and then **left** again along Church Close to the car park.

Walk 2 Off Broadway

This page (clockwise): Bourton-on-the-Water; Sudeley Castle; Broadway; Cotswold Way signpost
Opposite (clockwise): *Still Water* statue, Cirencester Park; Chalford; Arlington Row

WALK 3

SUDELEY CASTLE

Once a Roman hamlet and then an important Anglo-Saxon town with its own abbey, Winchcombe still possesses many timber-framed buildings dating back to medieval times. This walk gives a taste of the town before heading off to explore the grounds of Sudeley Castle, a fine 15th-century manor house that was once the home of Katherine Parr, the sixth wife of Henry VIII. The park is home to an array of trees planted in the 19th century by the family that saved the castle from ruin.

OS information
SP 025 284 Explorer OL45
Distance 1.6 miles / 2.6 km
Time 1¼ hours
Start/Finish Winchcombe
Parking GL54 5HX Bull Lane car park
Public toilets Back Lane long-stay car park, Winchcombe, GL54 5PZ; Sudeley Castle
Cafés/pubs Winchcombe; The Pavilion and picnic area at Sudeley Castle
Terrain Pavement, tarmac paths/drives and field paths
Hilliness Gently undulating
Footwear Year round
Public transport Frequent bus service to Winchcombe from Cheltenham: stagecoachbus.com

Did you know? On the night of 28 February 2021, Winchcombe became the site of a rare event: the arrival of a 4.6-billion-year-old carbonaceous chondrite meteorite. Scientists immediately put out an appeal for samples. The most famous were gathered up by Rob Wilcock, into whose driveway they had crashed. The 'Winchcombe Meteorite' was the first carbonaceous chondrite meteorite ever recovered in Britain. Some of its fragments can now be seen at Winchcombe Museum and London's Natural History Museum.

Local legend The ghosts said to haunt Sudeley Castle include a rather noisy blacksmith, a young boy and a friendly dog. However, the most impressive wraith is that of Janet, a former housekeeper at the castle, who keeps a critical eye on how things are run. She has been seen many times on the staircase or in one of the upper rooms 'running her finger disapprovingly over the furniture and alarming staff and visitors alike'.

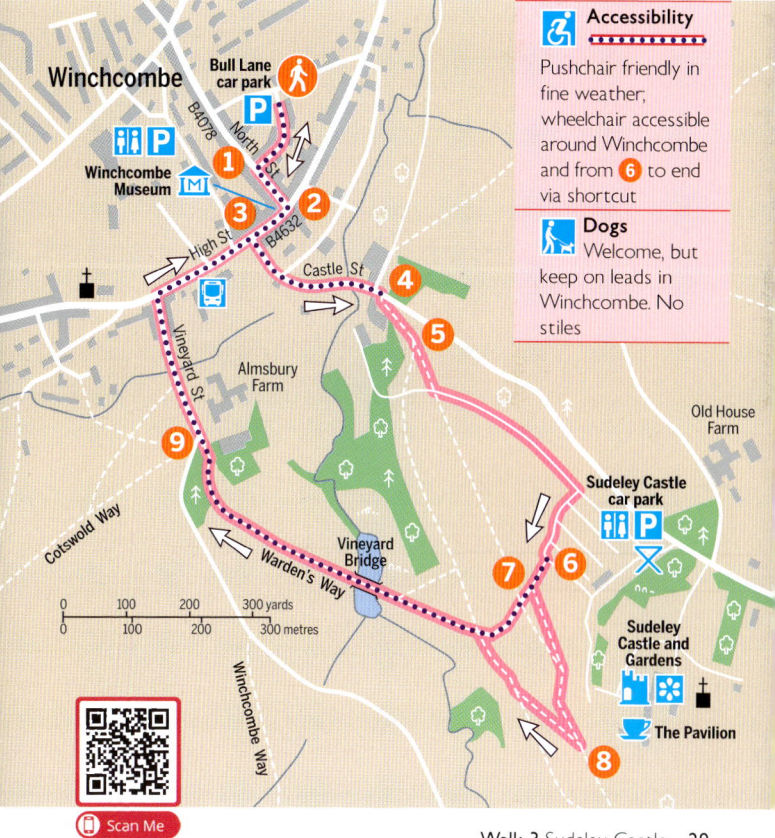

Walk 3 Sudeley Castle 29

STORIES BEHIND THE WALK

☆ **Queen Katherine Parr** 'Divorced, beheaded, died/Divorced, beheaded, survived' – so goes the rhyme recalling the fates of Henry VIII's wives. Katherine Parr was the sixth spouse and hence the lucky 'survivor'. Katherine was the first English queen to become a published author and some rare editions of her books are on display at Sudeley Castle, where she lived, gave birth and died aged 36. She is now buried there, making Sudeley England's only private castle to play host to the remains of a queen.

🏛 Winchcombe Museum

Portraying 'Life in a Cotswolds Town', the museum offers an impressive range of exhibits, ranging from arts and agriculture to trade and industry. There are Neolithic tools, an Iron Age cup, a fragment of the Winchcombe Meteorite (pictured above, with the finder – see page 29) and curious oddities such as a World War II field telephone discovered in the tower of a church (winchcombemuseum.org.uk).

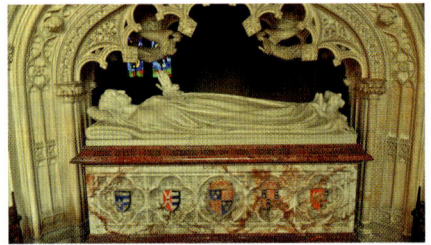

Bull Lane car park

■ Leave the car park via the pedestrian exit beside the map of Winchcombe and turn **right** to walk along Bull Lane to reach a T-junction.

1 ■ Turn **left** along North Street to reach another T-junction.

2 ■ Go **right** onto the High Street, passing the Winchcombe Museum, to meet Castle Street in 75 yards.

Gardens The first gardens at Sudeley were laid out by Ralph Boteler in the 15th century. Today, the castle runs to no fewer than ten different gardens. Visitors can wander around the Tudor Physic Garden to see the medicinal plants grown in the 16th century; the Ruins Garden, set in a portion of the castle slighted by Cromwell's army; the romantic Secret Garden, and seven more, each one changing with the seasons.

Sudeley Castle Constructed in 1443 on the site of an earlier fortified manor house, Sudeley Castle has a rich royal history. Richard III built a banqueting hall here; Henry VIII and Anne Boleyn stayed for five nights while the king planned the Dissolution of the Monasteries; and Elizabeth I visited on several occasions. The castle changed hands three times during the Civil War and on one occasion paid host to King Charles I himself (sudeleycastle.co.uk).

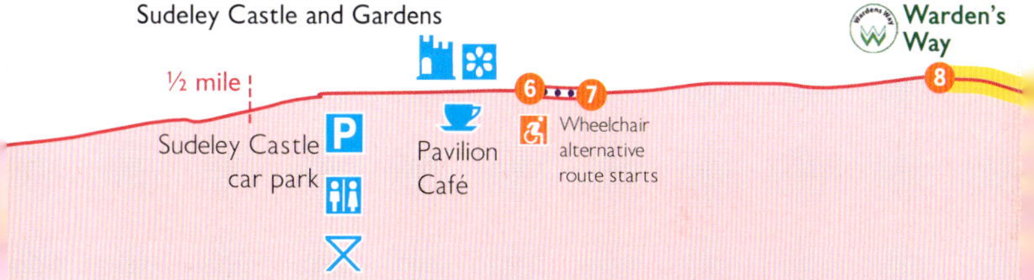

Sudeley Castle and Gardens

 Warden's Way

½ mile

Sudeley Castle car park

Pavilion Café

6 — 7

Wheelchair alternative route starts

8

3 ▶ Head **down** Castle Street.
▶ In 250 yards, rounding a bend in the road, watch for a fingerpost and a shallow flight of steps on the right.

4 ▶ Take to the footpath and go through the gate at the top of the steps.
▶ Keep **forward** for 75 yards to an unsigned path junction.

Walk 3 Sudeley Castle   31

NATURE NOTES

The parkland surrounding Sudeley Castle is full of mature trees, among them lime, oak, ash, beech, walnut and Atlas cedar. Many of these were planted in the 1800s by the Dent family.

You'll also see silver maple – one of the commoner trees in North America but whose relative scarcity this side of the Atlantic makes it seem rather more exotic. It can be easily identified by its leaves, which have the classic maple outline as seen on the Canadian flag.

Crossing Vineyard Bridge on Warden's Way (8 to 9), look out over the marshy lake which can be covered with hybrid cattails, more commonly know as reedmace or bulrush. The cigar-like seed head disintegrates to cotton wool-like fluff and thousands of individual seeds are dispersed by the wind.

The damp grassland around the lake is home to toads, their warty skin distinguishing them from smooth-skinned frogs, and slow worms, which are in fact legless lizards.

Heading back into Winchcombe, some of the walls you'll pass will be adorned with the lilac stars of trailing bellflower and great swathes of valerian.

Top left: toad
Top middle: bulrush
Top right: trailing bellflower
Bottom right: valerian

Warden's Way

Wheelchair alternative route ends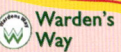

Vineyard Bridge

1 mile

5 ▪ At the junction go **left** and keep **ahead** when this soon joins a wide stony track leading to the castle car park.
▪ Either **cross** the car park to visit the castle or bear **right** to walk along the front of it.

6 ▪ At a small grassy roundabout, go straight **ahead** on a narrow roadway for 50 yards, passing a no entry sign on your right, to reach a gate on the left.

7 ▪ Go through the gate, signed Windrush Way, and pass under the walkway of a children's play castle and continue to a kissing-gate
▪ Go through the gate and aim for a small gate in the fence ahead, but do not go through it.

32 Short Walks Made Easy

Lime tree leaves

Vineyard Street — High Street — 1½ miles — Winchcombe Museum — Bull Lane car park

8 ▸ Instead, turn very sharp **right** on another grassy path – the Warden's Way – aiming to the right of a clump of trees to reach a gate in the far left-hand field corner.
▸ Pass through the hand gate and bear **left** onto a tarmac track, soon crossing Vineyard Bridge and continuing to a gatehouse.

9 ▸ Just after the gatehouse, upon reaching a public road, carry **straight on** along Vineyard Street.
▸ This leads to the High Street where you turn **right** to retrace your steps to the start.

Walk 3 Sudeley Castle

WALK 4

BOURTON-ON-THE-WATER

There's much to see and do in Bourton-on-the-Water but first you can enjoy this energising countryside stroll. Begin by following in a great composer's footsteps on the Gustav Holst Way. This takes you through a nature reserve to Wyck Rissington — apparently lost in time, it appears to be more meadow than actual village. The return to Bourton passes more meadows with a wonderful view to Little Rissington church, before a lovely lakeside path finale.

OS information
SP 169208
Explorer OL45

Distance
4.1 miles / 6.6 km

Time
2 hours

Start/Finish
Bourton-on-the-Water

Parking GL54 2LU
Bourton Vale car park, Station Road

Public toilets
Bourton Vale car park; Rissington Road car park

Cafés/pubs
Bourton-on-the-Water

Terrain
Field paths, stony tracks and lanes

Hilliness
Level or very gently undulating

Footwear
Spring/Autumn/Winter
Summer

34 Short Walks Made Easy

Public transport

Bus services 801, between Moreton-in-Marsh and Cheltenham; 802, from Kingham railway station; 855, circular to Northleach and Cirencester: pulhamscoaches.com

Accessibility

Wheelchair and pushchair friendly from 🚶 to ②, ④ to ⑤ (in Wyck Rissington), and ⑧ to end

Dogs

Welcome but keep on leads. No stiles

Did you know? Every August bank holiday, Bourton-on-the-Water stages a game of football in the shallow and usually tranquil River Windrush. The event is now over 100 years old and is played by two teams of six from Bourton Rovers FC. Large crowds cheer from the riverbanks and frequently get soaked in the process.

Local legend In 1954, Bourton-on-the-Water became home to the Museum of Witchcraft, based in a building known as Witches Mill. Founded by a Neopagan Warlock (and screenwriter) named Cecil Williamson, it housed numerous objects used in folk magic, Wicca and Freemasonry. However, it met with much local opposition, culminating in an arson attack. As a result, in 1960, the museum moved to Boscastle in Cornwall.

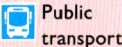

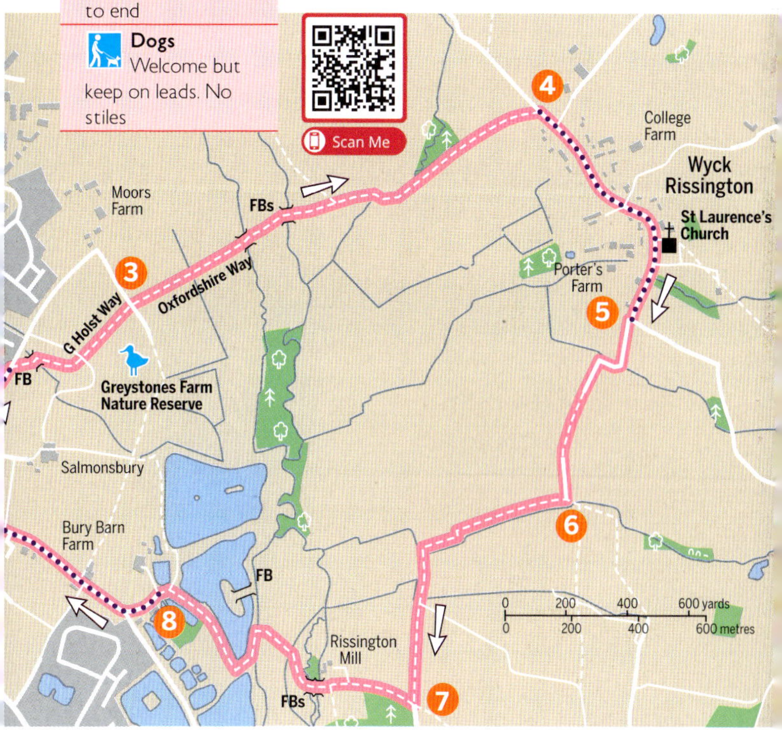

Walk 4 Bourton-on-the-Water 35

STORIES BEHIND THE WALK

☆ **Model Village** Built of genuine Cotswold stone at 1:9 scale, the model shows Bourton-on-the-Water as it stood in the 1930s but with the current shops, banks, etc., that inhabit the buildings today. It's so detailed it even includes a model of the model village. And such is its importance as a cultural artefact, it's now been awarded Grade II-listed status, just like some of the buildings it depicts (theoldnewinn.co.uk/model-village).

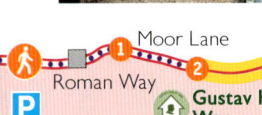

Cotswold Motoring Museum & Toy Collection

This museum is a must for anyone who likes looking at old cars, motorbikes and caravans, or heading down memory lane via childhood toys and games. There are vintage motors, model aeroplanes, toy boats, board games, and much more on show. Founded in the 1970s by a collector called Mike Cavanagh, the museum is housed in a delightful 18th-century mill (cotswoldmotoringmuseum.co.uk).

Bourton Vale car park

- Leave the car park to the left of the petrol station.
- Cross the road, turn **left** along the pavement and go first **right** along Roman Way.
- Walk to Moor Lane on the right in 100 yards.

1 ▶ Turn **right** along Moor Lane following the Oxfordshire Way for 175 yards to the first footpath on the right.

36 Short Walks Made Easy

☆ Windrush and its bridges

Bourton-on-the-Water is unusual for a village in having a river run right through the heart of it. This is due to the river being diverted in the 17th century to power three mills. Five picturesque stone bridges now span the river, the oldest of them being the Mill Bridge which was constructed in 1654. The others are the High Bridge (1756), Paynes Bridge (1776), New Bridge (1911) and Coronation Bridge (1953).

☆ Birdland Park & Gardens

Located in nine acres of woodland and gardens, the park has 50 different habitats hosting all manner of birds from pelicans and penguins to finches and flamingos. With a focus on conservation, Birdland is also home to lizards, snakes and a species of poisonous frog. You can go back in time too – there are velociraptors, a brachiosaurus and a tyrannosaurus rex lurking in the woods, which is unusual, even for the Cotswolds (birdland.co.uk).

Wyck Rissington
St Laurence's Church
1½ miles
2 miles

2 ➤ Pass through the metal kissing-gate in the hedge and follow a cross-field path – the Gustav Holst Way – to meet a tree-lined track in ¼ mile.

3 ➤ At the track, head **straight across** through two gates.
➤ Now back on the Oxfordshire Way, follow the path for ¾ mile, ignoring side paths and crossing a few water channels to meet a lane.

4 ➤ Turn **right** to pass through Wyck Rissington, following the lane to a sharp left bend about 300 yards beyond the church.

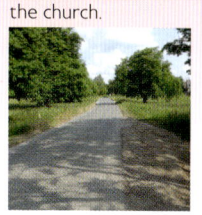

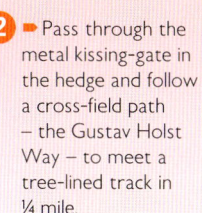

Walk 4 Bourton-on-the-Water 37

NATURE NOTES

This walk passes through Greystones Farm Nature Reserve, a site whose former meadows – lost when ploughed up in the 1980s – are now being restored by the Gloucestershire Wildlife Trust. The village of Wyck Rissington also has a glorious meadow at its heart, while the church at Little Rissington makes for a pleasing backdrop to yet more meadowland.

The meadows are full of plants such as lady's bedstraw, creeping buttercup and white clover, much loved by bumblebees.

While admiring this vibrant habitat, keep an eye out for the plants in the hedgerows at the meadows' edge. The delicate lilac blooms of germander speedwell, the pink (confusingly, not red) flowers of red campion, the purple spikes of hedge woundwort – used by apothecaries for centuries for its wound-healing powers.

Also seen in the hedgerows, elder is a small deciduous tree whose 'cushions' of creamy white

Above: Yorkshire fog
Middle: common blue
Below: marbled white

5 ▬ At the bend, leave the lane by going **straight on** along a stony track.
▬ Continue **ahead** through two gates as the path gets grassier to reach a bridleway T-junction in just over ⅓ mile.

6 ▬ At the junction, turn **right** through a gate to walk alongside a high hedge with fields to your right.
▬ Continue through meadows as the path swings 90 degrees left, going on to reach a wooden gate in 500 yards.

38 Short Walks Made Easy

flowers in May, used to make elderflower cordial, are followed by dense clusters of purple-black berries in late summer.

Meadow butterflies seen in summer may include meadow brown, marbled white and common blue.

Above: dog roses
Below: elderflowers

Meadow at Greystones Farm Nature Reserve

Lakes
⑧ 3½ miles
Cemetery Lane
4 miles

Bourton Vale car park

⑦ ▶ Go through the gate and turn immediately **right** onto a stony track.
▶ The footpath goes through a gap in a hedge, passes Rissington Mill and heads round a lake to a track T-junction.

⑧ ▶ Turn **left** along a wide track that soon becomes a lane.
▶ Stay on the lane to the main road and there turn **left** to retrace your steps to the start.

Walk 4 Bourton-on-the-Water 39

40

Opposite (clockwise): common sorrel; speckled wood butterfly; pink hawthorn
This page (clockwise): belted Galloway cows; meadowland; trailing bellflower; greater horseshoe bats

WALK 5

CORNBURY PARK

They do like a festival in this corner of the Cotswolds. This walk joins the village of Finstock (which hosts the Finstock Festival), through Cornbury Park (the venue for the Wilderness Festival) and finishes in Charlbury, which stages its own beer festival. Along the way you may see some of the deer that live in Cornbury Park, and you will pass through two fine avenues of trees. To begin this linear route, take the train (or drive) to Charlbury and hop on a bus to Finstock.

OS information

SP 361166
Explorer 180

Distance
2.1 miles/3.3km

Time
1 hour

Start Finstock, at the village shop bus stop
Finish Charlbury, at bus stop in Church Street

Parking OX7 3PQ Spendlove Centre car park, Enstone Road, Charlbury

Public toilets
Spendlove Centre

Cafés/pubs
Cafés and pubs in Charlbury; pub in Finstock

Terrain
Lanes; estate drives and tracks; grassy paths

Hilliness
Gently undulating

Footwear
Year round

42 Short Walks Made Easy

Public transport

Charlbury and Finstock are served by train services between Oxford and Evesham: thetrainline.com; from Church St, Charlbury, the X9 bus service (Witney to Chipping Norton) runs to the village shop, Finstock; bus service S3 runs between Oxford and Charlbury: stagecoachbus.com

Accessibility

Only suitable for wheelchairs and pushchairs around Charlbury

Dogs

Welcome, but keep on lead on shared-use cycle path ④ to ⑥. One stile

Local legend Each Palm Sunday, the inhabitants of several Oxfordshire villages take part in a long-standing and unusual tradition. They go on a walk to collect water from Cornbury Park's Wort's Well and Chalybeate Well, both of which are normally out of bounds. They mix the water with liquorice, brown sugar and a black peppermint to produce a cure-all called Spanish Liquor. The rite is believed to stem from the pagan Celtic worship of wells.

Did you know? In the past, if there was a fire in Charlbury, a man would rush around playing loudly on his bugle to warn the townsfolk. A fire at a farm in the 1870s was fought by women and children passing buckets of water from a pump. The Charlbury Volunteer Fire Brigade was eventually founded in 1881. Their engine was hauled by the firemen themselves. Only if the fire was outside Charlbury would some horses be found to pull it.

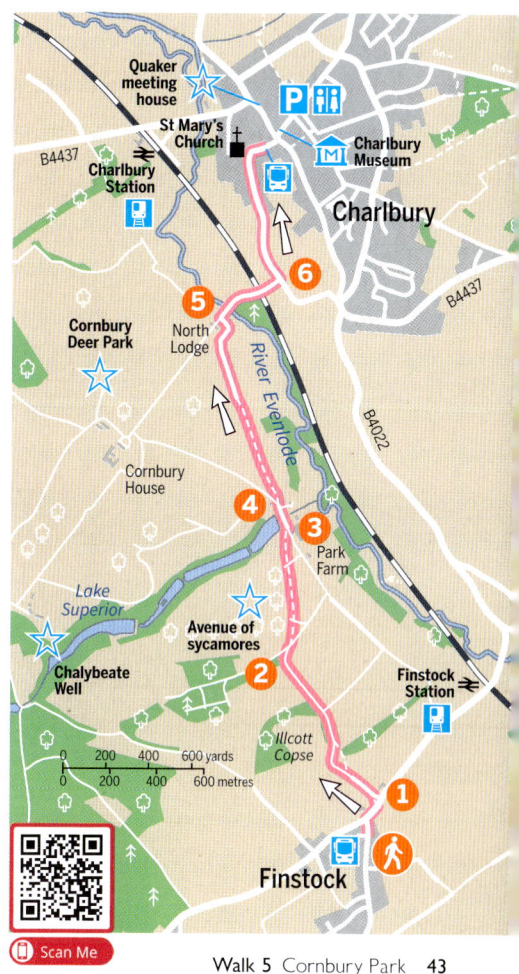

Walk 5 Cornbury Park 43

STORIES BEHIND THE WALK

☆ **The Gloveresses** For centuries, the villages on the edge of Wychwood Forest were known for their gloves, made at home from local deer hides by women known as gloveresses. By the 1850s, glove-making had become industrialised and Charlbury was the most important centre in the region. However, hundreds of gloveresses still worked in their cottages, with girls as young as five and women as old as 80 using their handiwork to make money. The last glove manufacturer moved away in 1968.

☆ **Cornbury Deer Park** It's apt that there's a deer park at Cornbury because the large woodland the estate contains – Wychwood Forest – is a small fragment of a once-immense royal hunting forest. In the park you might see the white-spotted chital deer; Dybowski's sika deer, which is only found in the far east of Russia in the wild; and fallow deer. Wychwood Forest, meanwhile, is home to fallow, roe and muntjac deer.

Hedgerow arch

½ mile

Village Shop, Finstock

- Catch the X9 bus in Church Street, Charlbury, for the five-minute ride to Finstock.
- From the bus stop outside Finstock's former post office, walk towards the main road and turn **right** for 75 yards to a stone stile on the left.

1
- Climb the stile and go through an arch in a high hedge.
- Immediately bear **right** across a lawn to a five-bar gate.
- Go through the gate and along a path across fields for ½ mile, using two more metal gates to meet an estate drive.

44   Short Walks Made Easy

☆ Quakers

Quakerism came to Charlbury soon after the movement was founded in 1654. The first ever female Quaker preacher, Anne Downer, was a daughter of the vicar at Charlbury and preached in her father's village. Quakerism took root and, despite persecution, a meeting house was eventually built in the 1680s. The one standing in Charlbury today is from the 1770s and it's a classic example of Quaker architecture, designed to reflect the movement's simple modest faith.

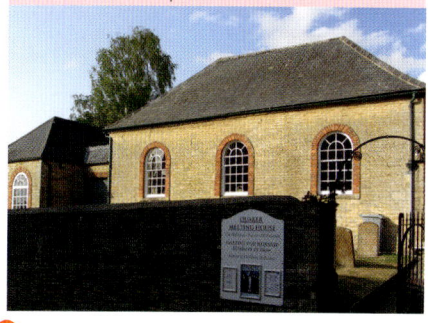

🏛 Charlbury Museum

Open at weekends and bank holidays, Charlbury's charming museum tells the story of this venerable market town. From the arrowheads left by Stone Age settlers to the marks left on the town by more recent Charlburians, all human life is here. The museum has an intriguing exhibition dedicated to objects unearthed in the town's houses and gardens and finds made by local metal detectorists. There's a peaceful garden to enjoy too (charlburymuseum.org.uk).

---

2 ➡ Bear **right** down the estate track, passing to the left of a low wall.
➡ Ignore the track crossing at a tangent, keeping **straight on** for ⅓ mile over grass, passing through an avenue of sycamores to meet an estate road.

3 ➡ At the road turn **left**, immediately passing a lake (left) and keeping **forward** to the gates ahead.

Walk 5 Cornbury Park   45

NATURE NOTES

One of the nature highlights of this walk is a superb avenue of sycamores. Often dismissed as a rather common and uninteresting tree (aside from its winged seeds, termed samaras, which 'helicopter' to the ground), it really comes into its own here. Refreshingly, there's also plenty of land beside the path that has been given over to wildflowers and grasses.

In early summer, the stunning purple flowers of pyramidal orchids may be seen.

Later in summer, there are crowds of bright and cheery ox-eye daisies, false oat grass swaying in the breeze and reams of dog roses.

Common teasels have found a home here too. Their spiky heads were once a vital tool in cloth-making, while their seeds form an important food source for goldfinches and other birds come the winter.

And of course don't forget to look out for fallow deer roaming Cornbury Park.

False oat grass     Hogweed    Sycamore samaras

4 ▬ Continue through a green gate marked National Cycle Network 442 and into a small field.
▬ Keep on this path for ½ mile, passing through a kissing-gate and, by North Lodge, a metal gate to reach another estate road 20 yards beyond.

5 ▬ Turn **right** along the tarmac to cross the River Evenlode and a railway line and pass through an avenue of tall lime trees to a road T-junction.

46   Short Walks Made Easy

Common teasels and ox-eye daisies

Goldfinch

Above: fallow deer
Below: pyramidal orchid

Railway　　　　　　　　　　　　　　　　　　St Mary's
　　　　　　　　⑥　　　　　　　　　　　　　Church
　　　　　　　　　　　　　　　　　　　2 miles
　　　　　　　　　　　　　　　　Church Street, Charlbury

⑥ ▶ At the junction, cross the road and turn **left**, walking along the pavement into Charlbury.

▶ The road bends right at Charlbury church to bring you back to the bus stop by the former Bell pub.

Walk 5 Cornbury Park   47

WALK 6

BLENHEIM PARK

Blenheim's 554-acre park contains a large lake, swathes of grassland and a copious number of trees. There are oak woods, Lebanese cedars, lines of tall poplars and a double avenue of limes to enjoy. Come in September and October and this circular walk round the park from neighbouring Woodstock will unveil a spectacular display of autumn colours. You'll also get a look at Blenheim Palace, a sort of English Versailles and one of the most opulent houses ever built.

CATCH A BUS

OS information
SP 446168
Explorer 180

Distance
4.1 miles/6.6km

Time
2 hours

Start/Finish
Woodstock

Parking OX20 1JF
Union Street car park, Hensington Road

Public toilets
Union Street car park

Cafés/pubs
Blenheim Palace; Woodstock

Terrain
Pavement, surfaced drives and grassy paths

Hilliness
Gently undulating

Footwear
Year round

48   Short Walks Made Easy

Public transport
Frequent bus services to Woodstock from Oxford and Chipping Norton: oxfordbus.co.uk; stagecoachbus.com

Accessibility
Wheelchair- and pushchair-friendly route on pavement/surfaced drives: 2.4 miles/3.9km; 1¼ hours

Dogs
Welcome but keep on leads. No stiles

Did you know? Sir Winston Churchill, the grandson of the 7th Duke of Marlborough, was born at Blenheim Palace. He maintained a close friendship with the 9th Duke and often spent time at Blenheim. When he died in 1965, Churchill was laid to rest within sight of the palace, at St Martin's churchyard in Bladon.

Local legend Almost inevitably for such a rambling edifice, Blenheim has a long history of paranormal activity. One of its ghosts even pre-dates the palace. A Roundhead soldier is said to walk up and down the corridors and warm himself by a bedroom fireplace. Some poltergeist activity has also been reported. Meanwhile, in the Dean Jones room – the most haunted location at Blenheim – a phantom chaplain has been seen sitting and reading his Bible.

Walk 6 Blenheim Park

STORIES BEHIND THE WALK

The Oxfordshire Museum There's a head-spinning range of subjects covered in the ten galleries of Woodstock's Oxfordshire Museum, each helping to tell the story of the county, its inhabitants and wildlife over the last 500,000 years. Dinosaurs are represented, as are Romans, Anglo-Saxons, Victorians (and indeed, Victoria herself), working people through the ages, the flora and fauna of the woodlands and more besides. And there's a café too, which is seldom a bad thing (oxfordshire.gov.uk).

☆ **Capability Brown** Lancelot 'Capability' Brown is thought to have designed more than 170 parks over his lifetime, but few of them as spectacular as that at Blenheim Palace. Commissioned by the 4th Duke of Marlborough in 1763, Brown's ambitious landscaping took a full ten years to complete. By building two dams he brought a 40-acre lake into being. Belts of trees and new drives created a regal setting for the lavish stately home.

☆ **Blenheim Park**

Union Street car park
► Leave by the car park's pedestrian exit (over to the left-hand side with your back to the vehicle entrance off Hensington Road), and turn **right** into Union Street.
► Walk to the T-junction in 175 yards.

① ► At the T-junction, turn **left** along Brook Hill. Ignore the left turn of Upper Brook Hill to reach the main road in 350 yards.

② ► Turn **right** along the main road.
► Go **over** the zebra crossing shortly afterwards and continue 20 yards along the pavement to go through a green gate to your **left** then, just before a domestic garage, turn **left** through another green gate.

50 Short Walks Made Easy

🏠 Blenheim Palace

Built between 1705 and 1722, this immense pile was intended as a royal thank you to the 1st Duke of Marlborough for his military victories. One of Britain's largest houses, the palace impresses with its sheer scale but its English Baroque style split public opinion at the time and dealt a blow to the reputation of its architect, Sir John Vanbrugh (blenheimpalace.com).

☆ **Marlborough Maze** Set in the walled gardens of Blenheim Palace, the maze is a whopping two miles long, making it the second largest hedge maze on the planet. Consisting of hundreds of yew trees, it's designed as a picture and contains spears, banners, trumpets, a cannon and piles of cannon balls. These all celebrate the 1st Duke of Marlborough's victory at the Battle of Blenheim in the War of the Spanish Succession in 1704.

| Ditchley Drive | ⑤ Stile (with no fence/hedge) | ⑥ Stile (with no fence/hedge) | 1½ miles — Great Park | ⑦ Park Farm | 2 miles |

☆ **Blenheim Park**

③ ➤ Take the surfaced drive to the **right**, beside a lake (Queen Pool), following it for ¼ mile to a driveway junction.

④ ➤ At the junction, for the all-surfaced route, turn **left** and re-join the route at ⑧.

➤ Otherwise, keep **right** for almost ½ mile to reach the middle of the spectacular tree-lined Ditchley Drive. Here you can short-cut left past the Column of Victory to continue the route from ⑧, or bend **right** with the drive and follow it for another 375 yards to a stile.

Walk 6 Blenheim Park 51

NATURE NOTES

The trees at Blenheim Park are spectacular. Two species to look out for are the columnar and elegant poplar, and the beech, with its smooth bark and its distinctive beechnuts, also known as mast.

In summer, across the grassland, what may at first appear to be dandelions could, on closer inspection, be hawksbeard. It adds a splash of gold to the pink-and-white candy stripes of field bindweed. It's a little known fact that this trumpet-flowered lover of neglected places is not only the bane of gardeners but is poisonous to mice.

Capability Brown's lake is home to a flock of greylag geese that can often be seen contentedly grazing the grassy shoreline. Mallards too seem unconcerned by the presence of humans.

The great wildlife attraction at Blenheim is the brown hare. Keep your eyes peeled for them when the route passes through the grassland parts of the park.

Poplar trees

2½ miles

Blenheim Palace

3 miles

☆ **Blenheim Park**

8 Grand Bridge (Queen Pool, left; The Lake, right)

5 ▬ At the stile to your left, with no fence or hedge on either side, bear **half-left** through the trees. There is only a faint path.

▬ Once through the trees, aim for another lonely and fenceless stile in 200 yards.

6 ▬ At the stile, bear **left**, aiming for the right-hand side of a large clump of trees (again, there is little or no path).

▬ Continue past the trees, bearing slightly **left** and aiming for a distant farmhouse. Leave the field via a kissing-gate at Park Farm.

52 Short Walks Made Easy

Greylag geese

Hawksbeard

Above: beechnuts
Below: brown hare

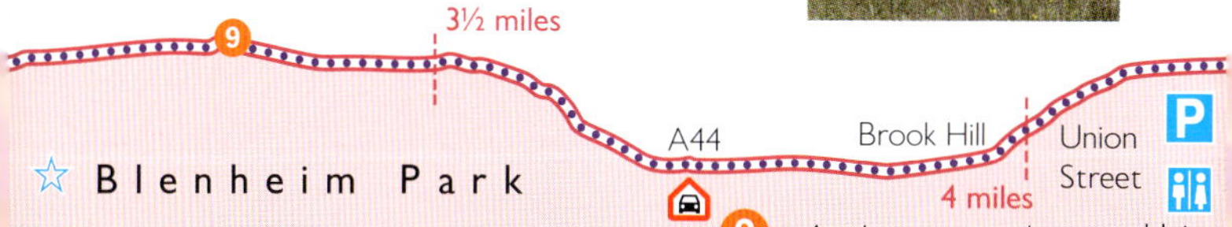

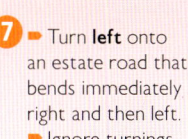

☆ Blenheim Park

3½ miles

A44 Brook Hill Union Street

4 miles

Union Street car park

7 ▸ Turn **left** onto an estate road that bends immediately right and then left.
▸ Ignore turnings to the right and continue to Vanbrugh's Grand Bridge in 1 mile.

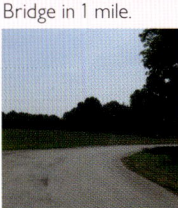

8 ▸ **Cross** the bridge and turn **left** in front of the palace gates along a wide tarmac path.
▸ Follow this as it curves left and away from the palace to the next crossways in 225 yards.

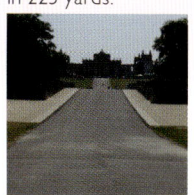

9 ▸ At the crossroads, turn **left** towards a distant arch.
▸ Bend with the drive to the left of the arch and walk down towards the gate you came in by.
▸ Turn **right** through the gate and retrace your steps to the car park.

Walk 6 Blenheim Park   53

WALK 7

BIBURY

CATCH A BUS

OS information
SP 114068
Explorer OL45

Distance
1.8 miles/2.9km

Time
1 hour

Start/Finish
Bibury

Parking GL7 5NL
Village lay-by, opposite Bibury Trout Farm

Public toilets
The Street, Bibury (by bus stop)

Cafés/pubs
The Swan Hotel; The Catherine Wheel pub

Terrain
Pavement, lanes and grassy paths

Influential designer and craftsman William Morris described Bibury as, 'the most beautiful village in England'. And to be fair, he had a point. With Cotswold stone cottages topped by roofs of handmade biscuit-coloured tiles, it is something of a dream. This walk explores the village and the paths around it, taking in a small stretch of the River Coln and some wonderfully picturesque mill buildings. It starts right opposite something very few villages can lay claim to nowadays: a trout farm.

54 Short Walks Made Easy

Hilliness	Mostly flat, with only gentle slopes
Footwear	Winter 🥾 Spring/Summer/Autumn 👟
🚌 **Public transport**	Bus service 855 between Bourton-on-the-Water and Cirencester: pulhamscoaches.com
♿ **Accessibility**	Wheelchair and pushchair friendly around Bibury and Arlington from 🚶 to ❺ and ❽ to end
🐕 **Dogs**	Welcome but keep on a lead. No stiles

Did you know? In 1992, the design for the first-class special-edition Christmas stamp (which then cost a mere 24p) was taken from a window in St Mary's Church at Bibury. Renowned stained-glass artist Karl Parsons (1884–1934) – a member of the Arts and Crafts movement (see page 16) – created the window for St Mary's in 1927. It shows the Virgin Mary in her traditional blue staring resolutely at the viewer while holding the baby Jesus.

Local legend The story of the Grey Lady, whose shade walks the Rack Isle Path in Bibury, is a rather pitiful one. She was a young woman called Mary who married a much older widower, the miller at Arlington Mill. One winter's evening he arrived home unexpectedly and discovered his wife and eldest son in flagrante. He hurled his progeny from a high window, killing him. He locked Mary out and she froze to death.

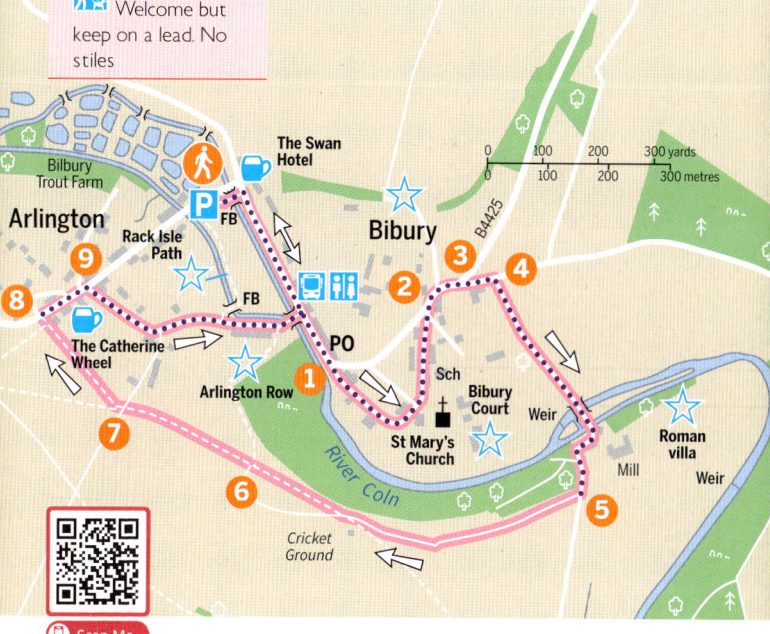

Walk 7 Bibury

STORIES BEHIND THE WALK

☆ **Bibury** Named 'Becheberie' in the Domesday Book, Bibury is home to a late-Saxon church that would have been quite new when William I's administrators called by. The bijou village appears little changed from its 17th-century days of cloth-making and fulling. Besieged by tourists in the summer, Bibury is best visited in the autumn when it's much quieter and the honey-stone cottages and the golden leaves of the trees appear to melt into one.

☆ **Arlington Row** Built in 1380, this is often claimed to be the most photographed row of cottages in Britain. Though it may be difficult to believe, given their perfection, they were not built as cottages at all but were a repository thrown up by local monks to store wool. It was only in the 17th century that the building was converted into cottages for weavers. Today they are lived in by (presumably very long-suffering) villagers.

The Swan Hotel (left)
Footbridge (River Coln)
Village lay-by, opposite Bibury Trout Farm

River Coln B4425

St Mary's Church
Bibury Court (beyond church)

B4425

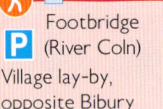

1
- Leave the lay-by at the river end to cross a footbridge and turn **right** along the pavement to walk beside the River Coln to the first turning on the right.

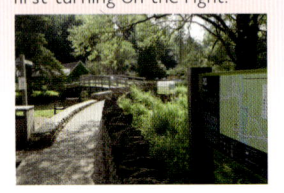

1
- As the road bends left, keep **ahead** down the side road.
- The road bends left, passing St Mary's Church (see page 55) and a school before leading back to the main village road (B4425).

56 Short Walks Made Easy

☆ Roman villa

Like many a Roman villa built in Britannia, the remains of the one on the outskirts of Bibury was discovered and then forgotten about until it was rediscovered centuries later. The owners had chosen a defensible spot for their rather grand home in a tight meander of the River Coln, which borders it on three sides. A mosaic floor unearthed in 1666 has sadly disappeared but Roman pottery and coins have since been found on the site.

☆ Bibury Court

On the River Coln, to the east of St Mary's Church, sits Bibury Court, a fine Grade I-listed Jacobean country house. Built between 1560 and 1599, it has been extended over the years, mostly by generations of the Sackville family. The grounds include a 17th-century mill house and an 18th-century dovecote. It was converted into an 18-room hotel in 1968 but a declining clientele led to its restoration as a private house in 2015.

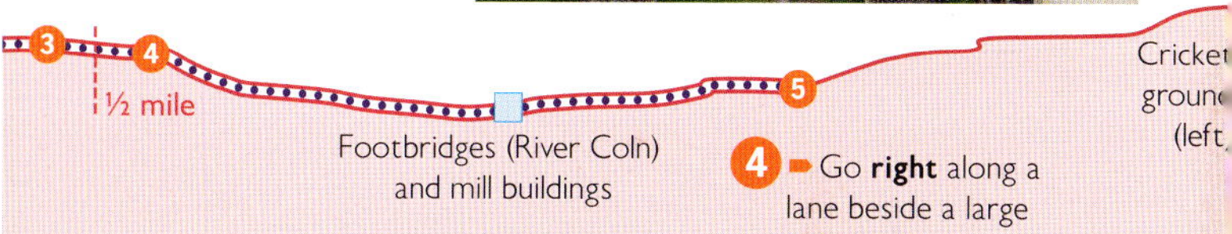

½ mile

Footbridges (River Coln) and mill buildings

Cricket ground (left)

2 ■ Turn **right** at the B4425 to walk along the pavement for 75 yards to a side road on the right.

3 ■ Fork **right** onto a road signed Coln St Aldwyns/ Quenington/ Hatherop.
■ Walk 50 yards to a turning on the right.

4 ■ Go **right** along a lane beside a large field on the left.
■ Follow the lane over a bridge (River Coln), and pass between some venerable mill buildings and up a short incline to a gate.

Walk 7 Bibury 57

NATURE NOTES

The River Coln threads its way through the centre of Bibury and Arlington. If you see a flash of orange and electric blue zipping above the waters, that'll be a kingfisher hunting.

You could easily spot a heron too, either standing motionless like a statue or stalking the river and its banks for small fish and amphibians. The village's trout farm must always be on its guard! In flight, herons draw in their long necks but trail their long legs.

Water voles travel rather more sedately across the river, sometimes hiding themselves away amid the stands of yellow flag iris.

In the fields around the village you might encounter Zwartbles sheep, an attractive breed introduced to Britain from Friesland in the Netherlands in the 1990s.

At the edges of the fields, look for meadow crane's bill, a geranium with flowers divided into five light-violet petals.

Grey heron

Cricket ground (left) | 1 mile

5 ▶ Go through the gate and turn **right**, along a wide stone and grass footpath.
▶ Follow this through a gate and a field, passing to the right of a cricket ground to reach a kissing-gate beneath trees.

6 ▶ Go through the gate and continue along a track, ignoring a path to your right.
▶ Stay on this track until it bends sharply to the left, with a hand gate to the right.

58   Short Walks Made Easy

Above: Zwartbles sheep
Below: kingfisher

Top: water vole
Bottom: meadow crane's bill

The Catherine Wheel — Arlington Row (left) — Rack Isle Path (left) — 1½ miles — The Swan Hotel (left), Footbridge (River Coln) — River Coln B4425 — Village lay-by, opposite Bibury Trout Farm

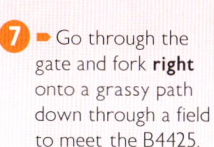

7 ▶ Go through the gate and fork **right** onto a grassy path down through a field to meet the B4425.

8 ▶ At the road turn **right** to pass The Catherine Wheel and reach a lane on the right (Hawkers Hill) just after the pub.

9 ▶ Turn **right** along the lane. In 150 yards, fork **left** (ignore private road, right) and drop down Awkward Hill to the cottages at Arlington Row (see page 56).
▶ **Re-cross** the river at the end of the lane and turn **left** back to the start.

Walk 7 Bibury 59

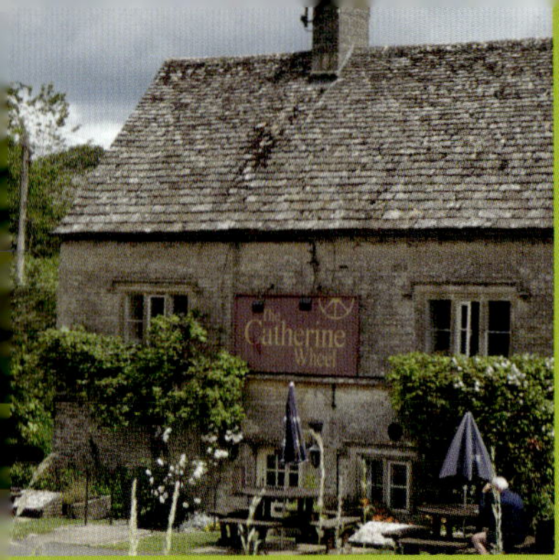
The Catherine Wheel
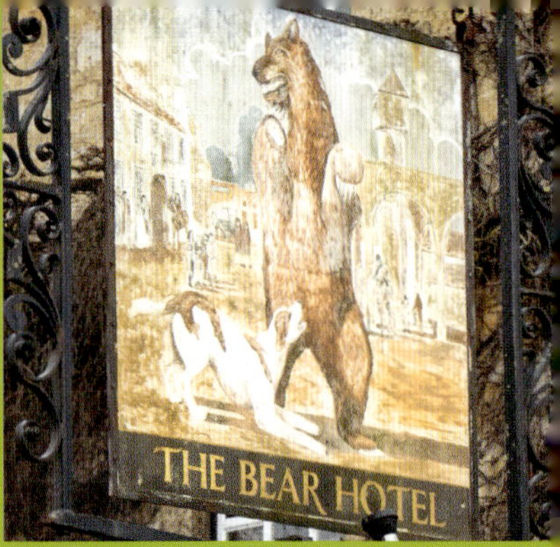
THE BEAR HOTEL
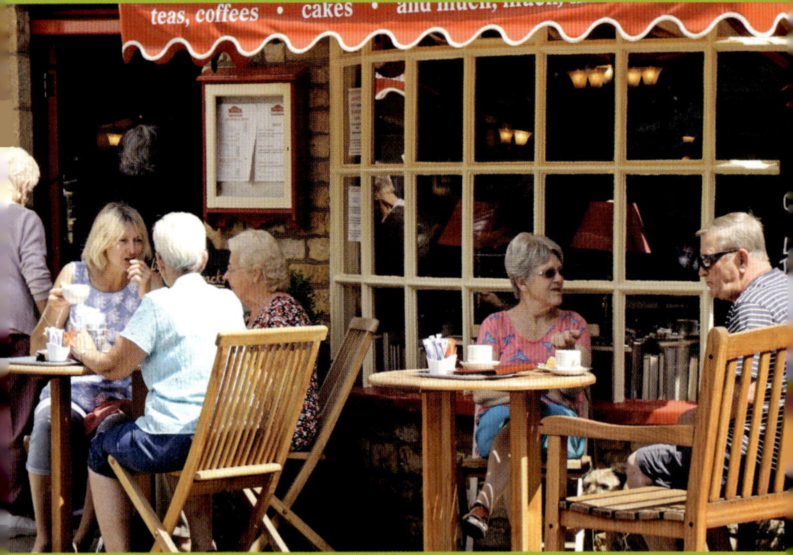
teas, coffees • cakes •
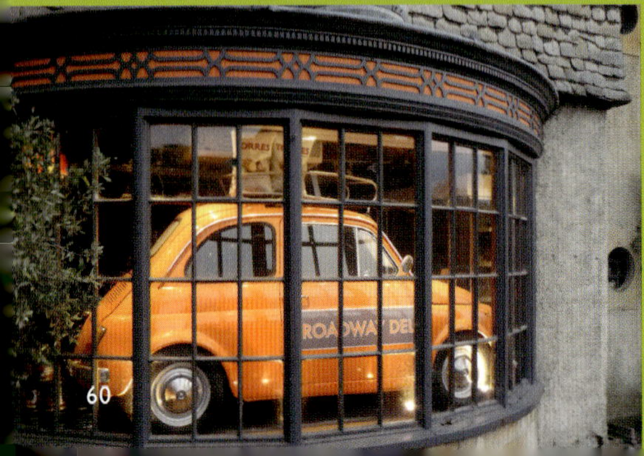
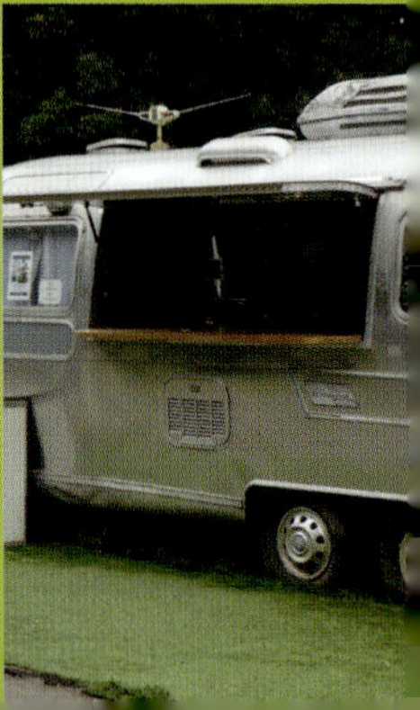

Opposite (clockwise):
The Catherine Wheel,
Bibury; The Bear Hotel,
Woodstock; a café scene
in Bourton-on-the-Water;
Beano in the Park,
Cirencester Park;
Broadway Deli, Broadway
This page (clockwise):
Lavender Bakehouse
& Coffee Shop, Chalford;
Cotswold honey

WALK 8

CIRENCESTER PARK

Cirencester Park forms part of an estate of around 15,000 acres that has been held by the same family for over 300 years. Nowadays, the park is open to the public every day from 8am to 5pm, free of charge. This walk heads briefly through the Roman town of Cirencester to explore a lovely corner of the park, passing a small folly and heading through a wood, before taking a long, lingering stroll down the magnificent Broad Ride.

CATCH A BUS

OS information
SP 021018
Explorer OL45

Distance
3 miles/4.8km

Time
1½ hours

Start/Finish
Cirencester

Parking GL7 1HN
Sheep Street car park

Public toilets
Brewery car park, GL7 1QX (150 yards east of 🚶 on far side of supermarket)

Cafés/pubs
Kiosk in Cirencester Park; Cirencester

Terrain
Pavement; tarmac drives; compacted earth paths

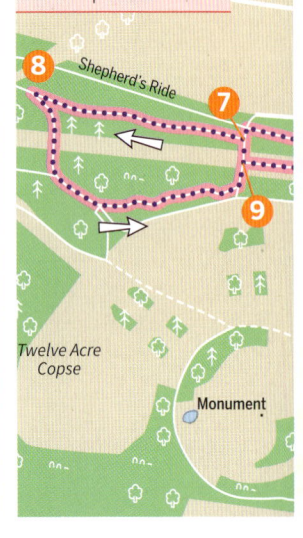

62 Short Walks Made Easy

Hilliness
Barely noticeable rise on the outward leg; corresponding descent on the return

Footwear
Year round

Public transport
Bus services 51 between Cheltenham and Swindon and 882 between Tetbury and Cirencester via Kemble Station: stagecoachbus.com

Accessibility
Suitable throughout for wheelchairs and pushchairs

Dogs Welcome but keep on leads. No stiles

Did you know? Cirencester Park saw service in both World Wars. In the Great War it became the HQ for the Warwickshire Yeomanry. In World War II it was the site of two extensive hospitals run by the US military. In July 1944, big band leader Glenn Miller played to 7,000 soldiers there, five months before the plane he was travelling in went missing en route to France.

Local legends Cirencester is reportedly home to a great many spectres and apparitions, from a sinister lady at the Black Horse pub and a faceless monk at the King's Head Hotel to a poltergeist that hurls books around the local branch of WH Smith. Cirencester Park itself is said to host the shade of a US Air Force pilot who talks to visitors but disappears after uttering his opening sentence.

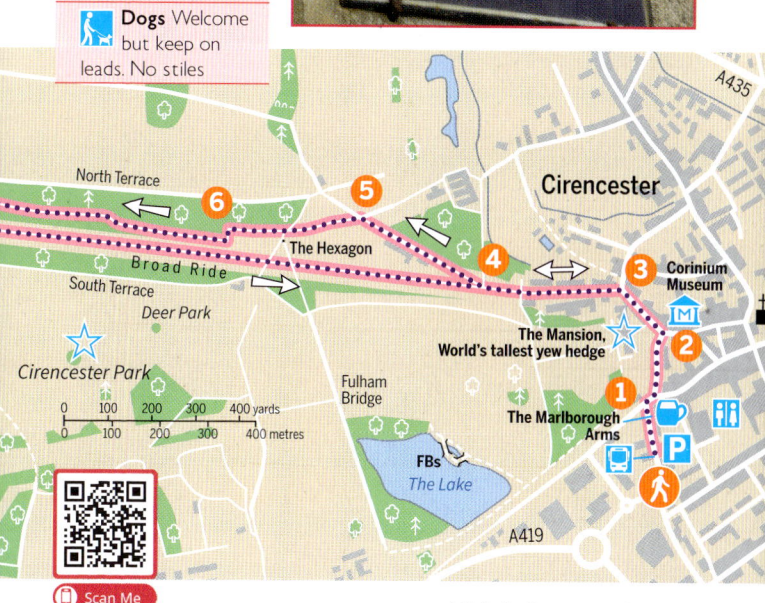

Walk 8 Cirencester Park

STORIES BEHIND THE WALK

☆ **Cirencester Park** Purchased by Sir Benjamin Bathurst in 1695 as a gift for his son Allen, Cirencester became one of the 18th-century's most grandiose and desirable parks. The 1st Earl added further neighbouring estates and joined them up with an avenue that stretches to Sapperton, five miles away. He also planted trees chosen to give colour and introduced fallow deer, a herd of which roams the park today (cirencesterpark.co.uk).

☆ **The Mansion** The stately home that sits in the park was built by Allen, the 1st Earl of Bathurst. He used the foundations of a Tudor-Jacobean house which itself may have been constructed on the ruins of Cirencester Castle, laid waste by King Stephen in 1142. To keep a certain distance between the house and the lesser abodes of the town's inhabitants, a natural barrier was planted which has since become the tallest yew hedge in the world.

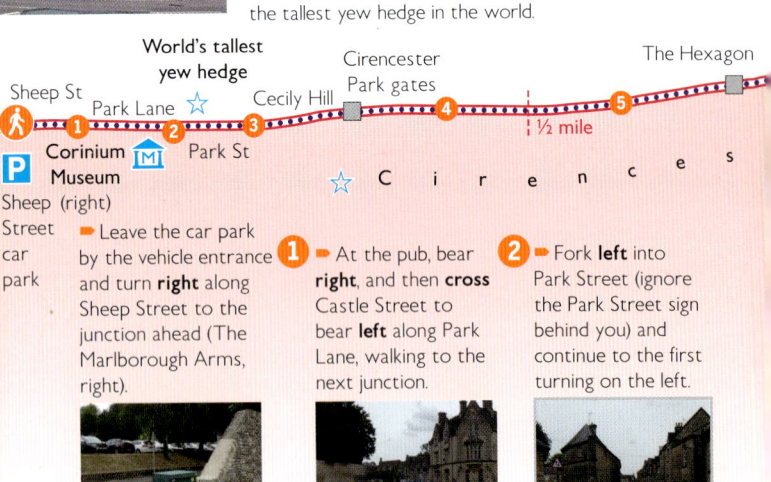

Sheep (right) Street car park

➡ Leave the car park by the vehicle entrance and turn **right** along Sheep Street to the junction ahead (The Marlborough Arms, right).

1 ➡ At the pub, bear **right**, and then **cross** Castle Street to bear **left** along Park Lane, walking to the next junction.

2 ➡ Fork **left** into Park Street (ignore the Park Street sign behind you) and continue to the first turning on the left.

64 Short Walks Made Easy

☆ **Alexander Pope** Although best known as the man who penned the mock-epic poem *The Rape of the Lock*, Pope was also keenly interested in gardens and architecture. A very good friend of the 1st Earl of Bathurst, he could often be found at Cirencester Park and collaborated enthusiastically in the nobleman's plans to transform it into one of the great English landscaped parks.

🏛 Corinium Museum

Cirencester's award-winning archaeology museum boldly declares that it contains '200,000 years of history'. It's especially good on artefacts discovered in what was the Roman town of Corinium (today's Cirencester), including a remarkable 11,000-coin hoard. There's some stunning gold and bronze from around 1300–1100BCE and a slew of money hidden in a lead pipe during the Civil War whose owner never came back to reclaim it (coriniummuseum.org).

Shortcut to ⑨, left

1 mile

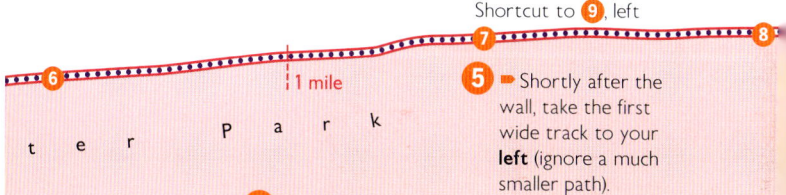

③ ▪ Go up Cecily Hill.
▪ At the end, enter the park through the ornate iron gates and keep **forward** for 100 yards to a fork.

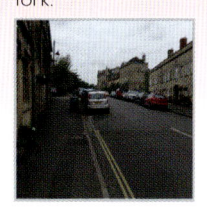

④ ▪ Bear **half right** along a wide tarmac path, ignoring the sharp right turn.
▪ Continue for 300 yards to the end of a low wall on your left.

⑤ ▪ Shortly after the wall, take the first wide track to your **left** (ignore a much smaller path).
▪ Continue **straight ahead** when you reach the Hexagon (stone folly) – *do not take the path that bends left around it* – to a woodland path fork in 125 yards.

Walk 8 Cirencester Park

NATURE NOTES

You'll find a good selection of trees in Cirencester Park, including some wonderful mature limes near the start of the walk.

As you pass through the woods, another deciduous tree species to look out for is the wild cherry, popular with the park's blackbirds and bullfinches for its abundant crop of fruit in late summer and autumn.

Most of Broad Ride is planted with horse chestnuts, a tree introduced to England from Turkey during the Elizabethan era. Although not related to the sweet chestnut, it was given the name because the seed casings are somewhat similar and, when ground to a powder, its conkers were given to horses to treat coughs.

Around the nettle and bramble patches in the parkland, keep an eye out for peacock and comma butterflies. The comma's upperside is a rich orange-brown and its wings have a distinctly jagged outline, with a small white 'comma' on its underside hind wing.

Outside the park, on Park Street (between ❷ and ❸), look up and you'll see the world's tallest yew hedge (see page 64).

Wild cherry

❻ ▰ Take the **left** (slightly indistinct) fork and enjoy the woodland trail for just over ⅓ mile to a junction with a blue sign, No Dogs Beyond this Point.

❼ ▰ At the sign, turn **left**.
▰ To shorten the walk, join the tarmac of Broad Ride to return to the park gate.
▰ Otherwise, follow the track round to the **right** to reach another dog sign in ¼ mile.

66 Short Walks Made Easy

Top left: blackbird
Above: horse chestnut flowers
Left: comma butterfly
Below: horse chestnut seed case and conkers

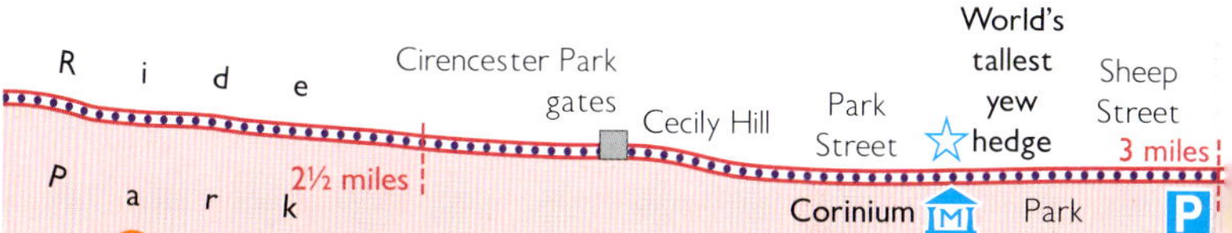

R i d e — Cirencester Park gates — Cecily Hill — Park Street — World's tallest yew hedge — Sheep Street — 3 miles

P a r k — 2½ miles — Corinium Museum (left) — Park Lane — Sheep Street car park

8 ➤ At the Please Keep Dogs on Leads sign, turn hard **left**, almost back on yourself, on a track that soon passes a small stone pillar.
➤ **Cross** Broad Ride into woods. Ignore forks off right to arrive back at Broad Ride in ¼ mile.

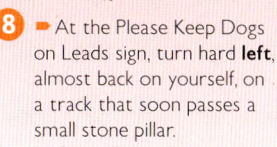

9 ➤ Regaining Broad Ride, turn **right** along it to return to the park entrance.
➤ Retrace your steps to the car park.

Walk 8 Cirencester Park 67

WALK 9

CATCH A BUS

CHALFORD

There's something of an Arcadian feel to the southern end of Chalford – the cottages dotted haphazardly here and there, clinging onto an absurdly steep hillside, possibly looking much as they did when the village was in its weaving heyday. This walk takes you out of the village along the abandoned Thames and Severn Canal to witness how the natural world has reclaimed the space. You return along an extremely quiet lane, and through woodland nature reserves, to enjoy sleepy Arcadia again.

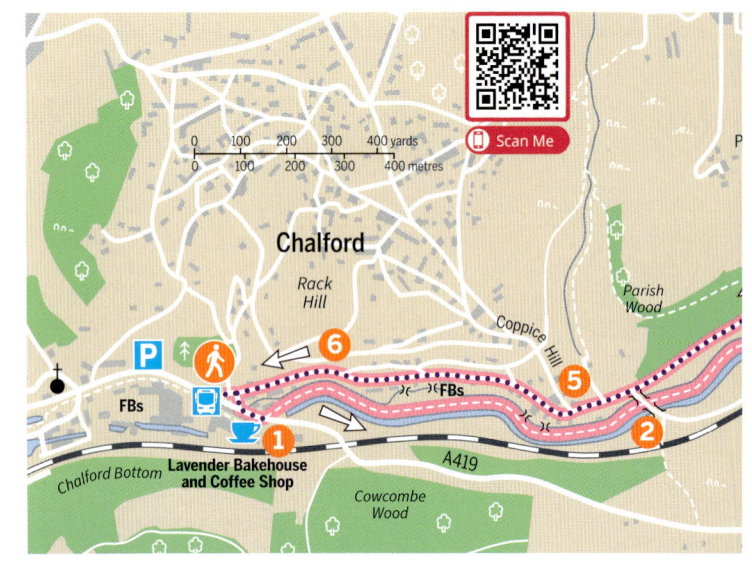

68 Short Walks Made Easy

OS information	Footwear
🚶 SO 895025 Explorer 168	Winter 🥾 Spring/Summer/Autumn 👟

Distance	🚌 Public transport
2.8 miles/4.6km	Frequent buses between Stroud and Cirencester operated by Cotswold Green: services 54, 54A, X54: Gloucestershire.gov.uk; service C66: stagecoachbus.com
Time 1½ hours	
Start/Finish Marle Hill bus stop, Chalford	
Parking GL6 8PP A419, London Road, long lay-by	
Public toilets None	♿ **Accessibility**
Cafés/pubs Lavender Bakehouse and Coffee Shop, London Road	Wheelchair and pushchair friendly in Chalford and on the lane from ③ to end; canal towpath uneven and narrow in places, sometimes muddy and prone to being overgrown
Terrain Lanes and canal towpath	
Hilliness Level throughout; steps at ③	🐕 **Dogs** Welcome but keep on leads on road sections. Footbridge with a low stile at each end at ③

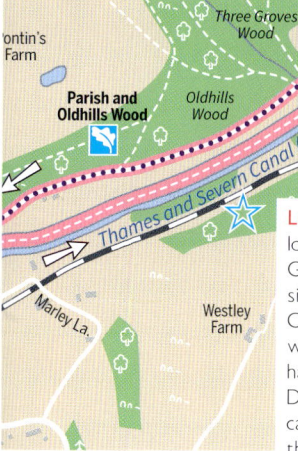

Local legend George and Dorcas Juggins were local legends in the first half of the last century. George wore a bowler hat and cravat, carried a silver-tipped cane and was known as the Charlie Chaplin of Chalford. His taciturn wife Dorcas wore extremely thick glasses and was apparently extremely handy with a hoe. Sadly, shortly after George died, Dorcas was killed when their two-room house caught fire, an event that caused a sensation at the time.

Walk 9 Chalford

STORIES BEHIND THE WALK

☆ Thames and Severn Canal

Chalford is home to the oldest section of the 28-mile Thames and Severn Canal which once linked England's two most important rivers. Those first four miles opened in 1785 and ran from Chalford to Wallbridge. Difficulties obtaining sufficient water supplies dogged the canal, and competition from the railways finished it off. The last vestiges were abandoned in 1941. However, the Cotswold Canal Trust has been gradually restoring sections and hopes one day to re-open it all.

☆ Long and round barrows

It's believed that Chalford and its surrounds have been occupied by humans more or less continuously for over 5,000 years. The earliest evidence of human activity has been the discovery of Stone Age flints. However, more obvious signs of settlement are the various barrows, or burial mounds, at Chalford Hill, France Lynch and Bussage. The most notable of these is a bowl barrow called Money Tump, about a mile north of the centre of Chalford.

☆ Thames and Severn Canal

½ mile — Marley Lane ②

Marle Hill bus stop; A419 lay-by parking, 75 yards west of bus stop

Lavender Bakehouse and Coffee Shop

➤ With your back to the bus shelter at the foot of Marle Hill, walk round the small grassy island and along the pavement beside London Road to Hallidays Mill Gallery in 100 yards.

① ➤ At the gallery, turn **left** along a footpath.
➤ Ignore left turns, including one signed to the Chalford Community Shop, and keep **forward** along an embankment with water on both sides to reach a canal bridge in ½ mile.

70 Short Walks Made Easy

Cloth-making For centuries the River Frome provided power to the inhabitants of Chalford, with the Domesday Book recording five mills there. The availability of sheep's wool, fuller's earth and teasels led to the construction of fulling mills in the Middle Ages. By the 17th century Chalford had become an important weaving centre, boosted by an influx of Flemish Huguenot refugees skilled in the craft. But by the late 1800s, economic factors brought an end to Chalford's cloth-making era.

Parish and Oldhills Wood

Covering nearly 40 acres, the Woodland Trust site of Parish and Oldhills Wood flanks the steep valley side above the canal and borders the lane used on the return leg of the walk. This ancient woodland consists mostly of beech but with some oak and ash and a varied understorey of hazel, holly and yew. In spring ramsons (wild garlic) and bluebells carpet the woodland floor while the canopy is a blaze of colour in autumn.

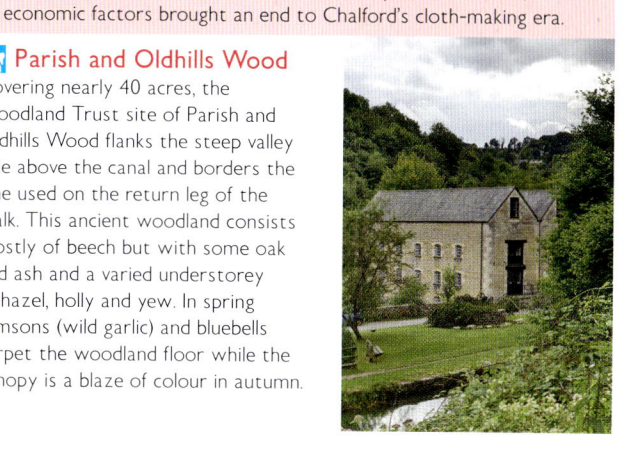

☆ Thames and Severn Canal

1 mile

2 ▰ Rise with the towpath to **cross** Marley Lane, bearing slightly **right** to continue along the narrow towpath, which soon becomes wider (with the abandoned canal, right) for ¾ mile to a footbridge.

3 ▰ On reaching the wooden footbridge, waymarked Thames and Severn Way and Chalford Biodiversity Trail, **cross** it and go up steps to turn **right** onto a lane.
▰ The road soon crosses the canal and arrives at a T-junction.

Walk 9 Chalford 71

NATURE NOTES

Nature famously abhors a vacuum. When the Thames and Severn finally closed, wildlife began to retake possession of the canal. What you'll experience on this walk is over 80 years' worth of that process.

The presence of water makes it an ideal spot for damselflies and dragonflies. They can be seen flitting about here in the summer months – particularly when they're energised by warm sunshine. Damselflies may be distinguished from dragonflies by their slender, more delicate appearance, and they rest with their wings closed; dragonflies have a swift and purposeful flight. Compare and contrast the emperor dragonfly and the common blue damselfly.

The well-vegetated canal is home to moorhens. They are shy but relatively easy-to-see birds that have red bills with yellow tips and green-yellow legs.

You'll also see larger plants tussling for space such as hogweed and common comfrey, the latter also known as knitbone for its use in healing fractures.

Grasses such as cock's-foot – so called because its flowers resemble the foot of a chicken – have taken up residence.

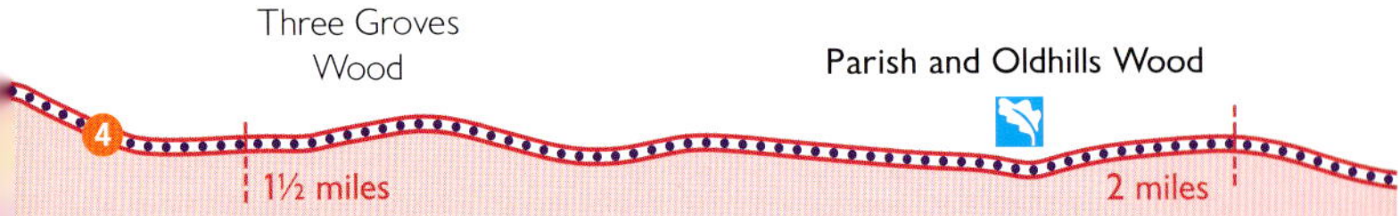

The canal (right) subsumed by nature

Three Groves Wood

Parish and Oldhills Wood

1½ miles

2 miles

4 ▬ Turn **left** along a gravel lane signed Chalford/Stroud.
▬ Soon becoming metalled, the lane takes you back to the edge of Chalford in almost 1 mile.
▬ Keep **ahead**, passing the first lane on the left to the next junction in 125 yards.

5 ▬ Ignore Coppice Hill to your right and keep **forward** on the road that becomes Chalford's narrow High Street. Look out for the spring to your right.

72   Short Walks Made Easy

Moorhen

Above: blue damselfly
Middle: emperor dragonfly
Bottom: cock's-foot grass

Coppice Hill ⑤

Marle Hill bus stop; A419 lay-by parking, ahead 75 yards

2½ miles

⑥ ➤ Continue down the winding High Street to return to the bus stop.

Did you know? Such was the size of Chalford's weaving boom in the 17th and 18th centuries (see page 71) that the village soon ran out of space for weavers' cottages. They were built instead on the steep slopes of Golden Valley. The paths to them were so slender and precipitous that donkeys had to be used to transport anything of weight. This practice died out as recently as the 1950s.

Walk 9 Chalford 73

WALK 10

WOODCHESTER PARK

Now owned by the National Trust, Woodchester Park is hidden away in a narrow valley and feels like a little world of its own. Sheep and cattle graze its pasture; bats flit about its ancient woodlands; and dragonflies skim the surface of its lakes. This foray into the depths of the park passes Woodchester Mansion (not NT), an ambitiously large Gothic house and chapel whose construction was begun in the 1850s but remains unfinished today.

OS information
SO 798 014
Explorer 168

Distance
3.5 miles/5.6km

Time
1¾ hours

Start/Finish
Woodchester Park

Parking GL10 3TS
Woodchester Park National Trust car park

Public toilets
Woodchester Mansion (on mansion open days only – see below)

Cafés/pubs
Woodchester Mansion café (not NT – open Friday–Sunday and bank holiday Mondays, April–October); picnic benches

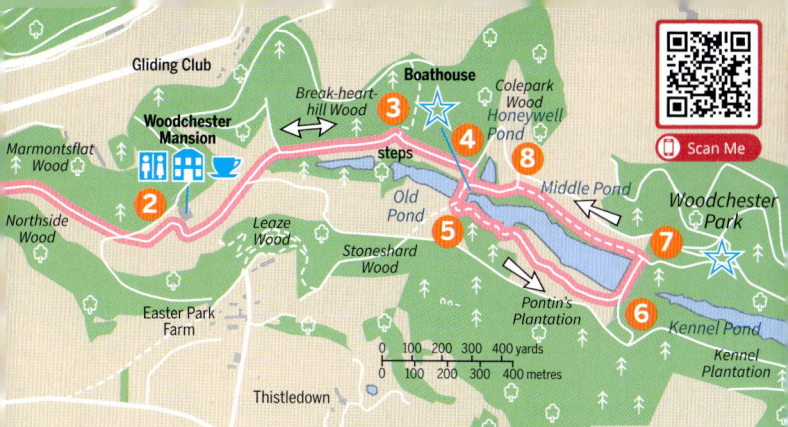

Terrain
Compacted earth and stony tracks; grassy paths

Hilliness
Gradual descent/ascent to/from the lakes

Footwear
Year round

Public transport
Bus service 65, between Stroud and Gloucester, stops at Nympsfield, ¾ mile south of 🚶: stagecoachbus.com

Accessibility
Flights of steps make this route unsuitable for wheelchairs; accessible for all-terrain pushchairs that could be carried down the steps

Dogs
Welcome but keep on a lead. No stiles

Did you know? A man whose products you will almost certainly have consumed was born in neighbouring Nympsfield in 1811. Alfred Bird was a pharmacist whose wife, Elizabeth, was allergic to eggs and yeast. Keen for her to enjoy custard, in 1837 he invented an egg-free version using cornflour. His Bird's Custard brand has since become known around the world. He later invented baking powder so that Elizabeth could eat yeast-free bread too.

Local legend Woodchester Mansion (see page 76) is a venue where a good many strange happenings have occurred. Its list of ghosts is impressive: a short man, a man trying to hide, another looking for someone, a girl, a young woman, an American pilot, a floating head and a horse-rider. Inexplicable music, noises, smells and sights have been recorded too. Unsurprisingly, it's possible to book a paranormal experience at Woodchester with a variety of different companies.

Walk 10 Woodchester Park 75

STORIES BEHIND THE WALK

🏠 **Woodchester Mansion** Seemingly lost in a wooded valley, this extraordinary French-flavoured Gothic Revival pile was never completed. Construction was started in the mid-1850s by one William Leigh and was still going in 1873 when he died. The mansion was passed down two generations until the family line died out. Still unfinished, it was eventually bought (and thus saved) in 1988 by Stroud District Council. Run by Woodchester Mansion Trust, it's open to the public (woodchestermansion.org.uk).

☆ **Woodchester at war** During World War II you'd have seen a very different park. However, unless you were one of the thousands of troops stationed there between 1939 and 1945 you wouldn't have seen it at all because security around it was extremely tight. The lakes you pass on the walk came in useful: soldiers used them to practise their bridge-building skills in preparation for the D-Day landings.

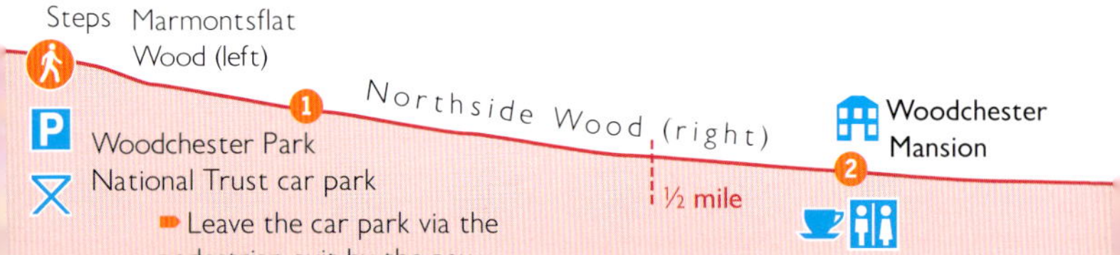

Steps Marmontsflat Wood (left)

Northside Wood (right)

Woodchester Park National Trust car park

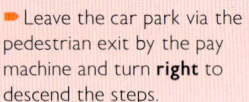

Woodchester Mansion

½ mile

- Leave the car park via the pedestrian exit by the pay machine and turn **right** to descend the steps.
- Turn **right** again at the bottom to follow the Mansion/Play Trail sign down a rough track to a junction in 375 yards.

❶ - Ignore paths up to the left and continue **ahead** following the Mansion/Boathouse signs and gently descending to a junction in front of the mansion in almost ½ mile.

76 Short Walks Made Easy

☆ Boathouse

Believed to have been constructed late in the 18th century, the boathouse predates the mansion. It was commissioned by the Ducie family when they occupied Spring Park, a house that was knocked down when Woodchester Mansion was built. Restored in 1998, it's popular with bats, which drop by here on their way to feed in the evenings. If you fancy taking a snap, the best angle is probably from the lake shore, between ⑤ and ⑥.

☆ Forest Green Rovers

The hamlet of Forest Green, on the eastern edge of Woodchester Park, lends its name to a rather remarkable football team. It was formed in 1889 by a local vicar, and once lost every single game in a season. However, in 2017, with Ecotricity co-founder Dale Vince as club chairman, Forest Green Rovers gained promotion to EFL League 2. This made Nailsworth (into which the hamlet has been subsumed) the smallest town ever to be represented in the football league.

Break-heart-hill Wood — Steps ③ Old Pond ④ ☆ Boathouse ⑤ Middle Pond ⑥
1 mile — Steps — 1½ miles

② ▸ At the junction fork **right**.
▸ Stay on the good, stony track for another ½ mile, following purple waymarks to the top of some steps, ignoring a path to the left en route.

③ ▸ Turn **right** to descend the flight of steps and continue to a crossroads in 300 yards.
▸ To view the boathouse, go **down** some steps.

Walk 10 Woodchester Park 77

NATURE NOTES

The fields to your right on your outward journey are often grazed by Jacob sheep, a piebald breed that can have up to four horns and was once an ornamental status symbol kept by wealthy landowners.

Tarry a while at the foot of the lake (between ❻ and ❼) in summer and you should see common club-rush, a sedge with dark green, sturdy stems and small, brown oval flower clusters, fringing the water. It was used to make baskets and for weaving into mats.

Flying over the water, if you're lucky, you may spot a black-tailed skimmer dragonfly. Males have pastel blue tails for much of their length, darkening at the tip, while females are yellow.

Greater and lesser horseshoe bats roost in the attics of Woodchester Mansion. Visitors can observe them from the bat observatory in the mansion via a high-definition, infra-red camera system rigged to relay close-up images of daytime activity in two different colonies.

Song thrushes are commonly seen and heard from the woodland rides and grassland trails.

Common poppy

❼ — Middle Pond — ❽ Honeywell Pond (right) / Boathouse — Old Pond (left) / Steps — Break-heart-hill Wood

2 miles — 2½ miles

❹ ▪ Otherwise, turn **right** on the main track to pass between two lakes. Reach the top of more steps in 35 yards.

❺ ▪ Turn **left** down the steps to head over a boardwalk and along the lakeside.
▪ The path leads through a kissing-gate and out into a field, on the far side of which, beyond two sets of gates, you reach a path junction.

78 Short Walks Made Easy

Top left: Jacob sheep
Above: black-tailed skimmer – female
Left: song thrush

Woodchester Mansion | Marmontsflat Wood (right) | Northside Wood (left) | Steps | National Trust car park

3 miles | 3½ miles

6 ▸ Turn **left** and walk beside the foot of the lake for 140 yards to a track junction.

7 ▸ At the T-junction, turn **left** in the Mansion/Play Trail/Car Park direction and continue for ¼ mile to the next T-junction.

8 ▸ Bear **left** at the fork, downhill, to pass a pond on your right, and keep **forward** to meet the crossroads by the boathouse.
▸ This time keep **ahead** to retrace your steps for the 1⅓ miles back to the start.

Walk 10 Woodchester Park

Publishing information

© Crown copyright 2024.
All rights reserved.

Ordnance Survey, OS, and the OS logos are registered trademarks, and OS Short Walks Made Easy is a trademark of Ordnance Survey Ltd.

© Crown copyright and database rights (2024) Ordnance Survey.

ISBN 978 0 319092 75 0
1st edition published by Ordnance Survey 2024.

www.ordnancesurvey.co.uk

While every care has been taken to ensure the accuracy of the route directions, the publishers cannot accept responsibility for errors or omissions, or for changes in details given. The countryside is not static: hedges and fences can be removed, stiles can be replaced by gates, field boundaries can alter, footpaths can be rerouted and changes in ownership can result in the closure or diversion of some concessionary paths. Also, paths that are easy and pleasant for walking in fine conditions may become slippery, muddy and difficult in wet weather.

If you find an inaccuracy in either the text or maps, please contact Ordnance Survey at os.uk/contact.

All rights reserved. No part of this publication may be reproduced, transmitted in any form or by any means, or stored in a retrieval system without either the prior written permission of the publisher, or in the case of reprographic reproduction a licence issued in accordance with the terms and licences issued by the CLA Ltd.

A catalogue record for this book is available from the British Library.

Milestone Publishing credits

Author: Dixe Wills

Series editor: Kevin Freeborn

Maps: Cosmographics

Design and Production: Patrick Dawson, Milestone Publishing

Printed in India by Replika Press Pvt. Ltd

MIX
Paper from responsible sources
FSC® C016779

Photography credits

Front cover: BkkPixel/Shutterstock.com.
Back cover: cornfield/Shutterstock.com.

All photographs supplied by the author ©Dixe Wills except page 6 Zoe Homes (Ordnance Survey); page 38 Kevin Freeborn; page 45 Quaker Meeting House in Charlbury by Gareth James, CC BY-SA 2.0, via Wikimedia Commons; page 75 Brian Robert Marshall / Gargoyle, The Mansion, Woodchester Park / CC BY-SA 2.0.

The following images were supplied by Shutterstock.com:-Page 1, 26 Simon Charles A Johnson; 3, 28 MyStockVideo; 5, 68, 70 John Corry; 7 Dave Turner; 9 JeniFoto; 13 PJ photography; 17 Mo Wu; 18 Wagner Campel; 19 Nigel Housden; 24 Alec Taylor; 26 Caron Badkin; 26 Craig Ballinger Photos; 26 David Hughes; 27 chrisatpps; 27 stocker1970; 30 elvisvaughn; 31 Gardens by Design; 33, 71 Martin Fowler; 33 Valsib; 36 chrisdorney; 36 Konmac; 37 Starsphinx; 41, 59 Rudmer Zwerver; 44 Toa55; 46 Gabriela Beres; 47 J Need; 47 Martin Prochazkacz; 57 Christian Mueller; 58 Robert Adami; 59 Ian Schofield; 60 Caron Badkin/; 60 Wildwater.tv; 61 Alena Veasey; 64 Colin Burdett; 64 Richard Whittle; 67 aaltair; 67 DmyTo; 67 Hajakely; 67 M. Schuppich; 73 Birute Vijeikiene; 73 iliuta goean; 73 Jeremy Burnside; 79 Joop Zandbergen; 79 Rasmus Holmboe Dahl.

80   Short Walks Made Easy